OCD: A LIFE IN TORMENT

Enduring a Lifetime of Obsessive-Compulsive Disorder

ψ

The disturbing result of intimate contact with the detail of reality or the macroscopic manifestation of quantum uncertainty? *(Back Cover)*

What do I mean?

The sentence tentatively alludes to the realm of quantum mechanics where the rules of classical Newtonian physics break down. At this infinitesimal scale, matter behaves in an uncertain, unpredictable manner, whereby events can only have a probability of occurring. Erwin Schrödinger's mathematical equation's universal probability wave function is given by the Greek letter psi (ψ).

When a particle exists in a quantum superposition state (itself alluding to the indecision of *enacting or ignoring* a compulsion), *observation* (synonymous to a *decision* employing willpower) collapses the superpositioned wave to either one outcome or the other to produce certainty (compulsion or non-compulsion).

Hence my light-hearted allusion, because OCD can be described as uncertain, chaotic and indecisive behaviour in the classical macroscopic realm and a *decision* produces the outcome by collapsing the indecision (probability wave).

In the following text I will occasionally make reference to quantum effects and analogy.

OCD: A LIFE IN TORMENT

Enduring a Lifetime of Obsessive-Compulsive Disorder

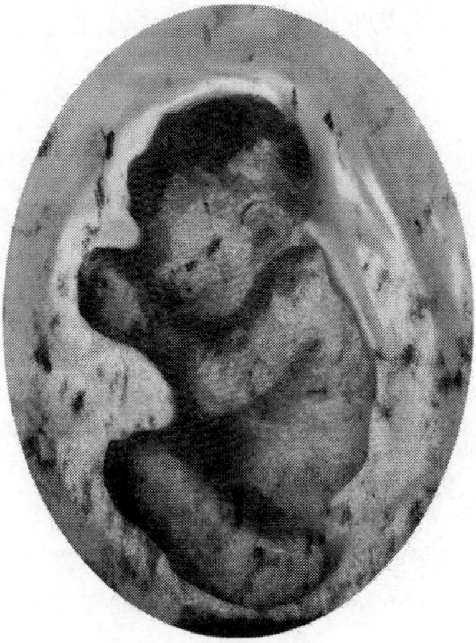

The Dark Embryo in a Cotton Coffin

Richard E Harding

OCD: A Life in Torment
Enduring a Lifetime of Obsessive-Compulsive Disorder

Font in Palatino Linotype 11 pt

ISBN 978-0-9574159-6-6

A CIP catalogue record for this book is available from the British Library.

Written, formatted, edited and published by

Richard E Harding B.Sc. (Hons) Biol, Geol.

Cover design by Richard E Harding

Cover image courtesy of pixabay.com

Embryo image after Leonardo da Vinci

Rattlesnake image courtesy of clipartlord.com

3D Depressed Man Sitting courtesy of Master Isolated Images

at FreeDigitalPhotos.net

Art Nouveau decorative images - Public Domain

CONTENTS

Getting through every minute of every day for a lifetime has been torture for me and I do not know how I have survived its devastation. I feel that I won't fear death because it will be a wonderful release from a joyless life of torment and misery.

Anxiety, OCD and benzodiazepine addiction has destroyed me and disallowed maintaining a close relationship with others. I suffer the demons of doubt and hesitation - dark doubt – dark dreams and nightmares - even doubting my own worth to exist.

The consequence of obsessive high resolution examination of reality's brightly lit complex landscape and the stark contrast of its surreal, deep, dark side, with its hidden monsters and demons that lurk in the shadows waiting to cancel out the light. The two inseparable faces of the reality of intelligent existence.

Richard E Harding, August 2016

OCD: A Life in Torment

For my children:
Timothy, Aimie, Matthew,
Jonathan, Julian & Nicholas,
in the hope they will understand

To Matthew and Louise
Thank you

CRÖTALUS
PUBLICATIONS

INTRODUCTION

ABOUT THIS BOOK

The idea for this book began life after I sent a letter to my daughter, Aimie, in 2002, in an attempt to explain in detail the agony I go through with obsessive-compulsive behaviour that has plagued my life for over sixty years. I hoped she might better understand the workings of OCD with a minute-by-minute account of the obsessive thoughts which result in tormenting compulsive rituals. That letter became chapter eight - Until It Feels Right – and very nearly the title for the book.

It has certainly been a cathartic experience over the past few years writing this book and vividly reliving my anxious life. I wanted to describe my ritual compulsions in all their grim detail to reveal all those long, unbearable, secret moments to my estranged children and to fellow sufferers who will identify and empathise with the bizarre behaviour and not feel they suffer alone. Also, to their families, who may at last, part-understand the unrelenting living hell we go through each day and night.

OCD is not just being fastidious and perfectionist, *unless it increases your anxiety to such a degree that it takes over your life.* It can manifest itself in many forms as your anxiety creates obsessive doubt and thought-cancelling ritual compulsions. We try to control our obsessive behaviour and not let it control us, otherwise the resulting compulsions quickly erode our confidence and compel us to doubt all we think and do. It insidiously takes over like a parasite and will eventually occupy and torture the remaining fragile shell which was once you, continuing to destroy your life as it has mine.

I describe my severe OCD as a continuous nervous breakdown because I think that best describes the experience, fuelled by near constant, uncontrollable anxiety and panic overflowing the limits of my endurance, but somehow forcing myself to keep on going during the interminable hours the compulsions consume and demand, that eat into my shredded sanity like waves tearing down coastal cliffs.

Although officially undiagnosed, I am certain I have Asperger's Syndrome, which I believe has been my saving grace. My fascination and love of scientific detail give me a reason to enjoy some moments of respite from OCD. For me, it is a gift to be aware of the details of reality and to be a deep thinker, despite the melancholy it inevitably induces.

Self-help books abound, so I hope this book may help on another level: that of revealing and sharing my detailed OCD experience, because I know it helps tremendously to identify with our strange, but all too familiar thoughts and behaviour. Employing OCD self-help is one of the most difficult acts of willpower to achieve; that is precisely why OC behaviour is so utterly difficult to stop – it's like a runaway train.

With the qualification of a life-time of bitter personal experience of most types of obsessive-compulsive behaviour, I will offer the following advice:

Firstly, you must reduce anxiety levels to a point where you can start to apply your willpower with some degree of confidence.

This may seem impossible, since the stress of enduring compulsions is of the highest order of anxiety and is self-perpetuating, but in my experience, once I'd achieved a comparatively stable home life in 2009 after decades of misery and despair, I was able to test my willpower against the OCD.

After successfully reducing or ending minor compulsions, the feeling of achievement is enough to point you on the right road. An example of minor compulsions would be not to straighten the edges of magazines and objects that are misaligned to our perfection-seeking minds. Feel proud that you have left them imperfect, because you know deep down in your heart-of-hearts that it is a positive signpost to your future well-being. The first time you attempt this will be agonisingly difficult, but believe me it can, *and must,* be done.

It is not something to put off until it 'feels right' tomorrow. Believe in yourself that NOW is the time to act.

You may, as I do, react to this compulsion-denial by face and body-twisting contortions, finding it almost impossible to move your feet in an attempt to escape the area of your compulsion.

But, you will know that you have a million fellow sufferers' heartfelt minds, including mine, urging you, encouraging you on, waiting to give you a well-earned cheer, for we know exactly what you're going through!

You are likely to be alone when you deny a compulsion; use this fact to your advantage to know that ***you are capable of this momentous step on your own.*** You do not need to be encouraged by hours of therapy talk and chart/form-filling. Take a couple of slow, deep breaths and exhalations and relax your shoulders to aid calmness and, as they say, ***feel the fear and do it anyway***.

You *will* feel anxious and panicky with the prospect that all you do, or try to do, after leaving the papers unstraightened or the ornament askew, will feel awkward and imperfect; but please trust me - ***facing the fear means the fear will fade***. The OC demon hates to be ignored. This is not a real demon of course, because demons do not exist - just in case the word *demon* bothers you! This is another unreasonable compulsion trigger to ignore, especially if you are religious. But, if you already believe in supernatural delusion, then you probably *do* believe in demons, angels and such like, and need to conquer *scrupulosity,* as it is called in religious OCD terminology.

My use of the word demon is just a useful metaphor to employ here, especially because historically it was thought that a demon had taken up residence in the afflicted person's body as the only explanation at that time before scientific reasoning for something that could force them to behave strangely against their will. Other examples would be epilepsy, bipolar disorder and heart attack.

Even after a relatively short time you will feel that the success of your compulsion-denial achievements outweigh worrying about them not being perfect. The fact that it is trivia will be more apparent to you - ***more real.*** Now for the exciting bit, ***and I genuinely mean exciting!***

Choose another minor compulsion to obliterate - like My Toilet Roll Rules! you will read about on page 118 (since overcome by not having a toilet roll holder!) I am able to leave the roll *not* millimetre-adjusted if I am *not* anxious, but I usually *am* very anxious after my Torture Chamber experience (page 58). But I will now work on it, especially since I have just said it is a *minor* compulsion!

The feeling of excitement builds when you begin to realise that you have actively denied several compulsive, tormenting trials. It actually feels good and propels you forward to envisage how much better you will feel about your vast achievements as you prove you can do it again and again. You will look forward to telling others of your successes and that if you continue to be strong enough and persist with your compulsion-denials, you have at last *given yourself the permission to be free from them*, and, most importantly, to be free from worrying that you *haven't* done the compulsions properly, or at all, as the 'demon' demands. ***But beware of complacency and don't let up on your vigilance for a minute,*** because the demon will be lurking nearby to catch you off guard, tempting you to give in to just one compulsion, like adjusting that askew ornament. Think of it remaining in that imperfect position as a 'fingers-up' to the demon. Leave it 'wrong', *and* the cushion, the loo mat *and* the toilet roll. However, I do draw the line at leaving a new toilet roll back-to-front on the holder (paper hanging against the wall) fitted by a well-meaning visitor; you have to draw the line at that! More humour, more stress relief, rather than anxious tension caused by a roll of paper!

I have recently used another trick to fool the OC*Demon*. During checking surfaces by scanning in fours or eights in the Torture Chamber, I deliberately allowed the inevitable compulsion restart intrusive image (or thought) to act as a blanking trigger. By this I mean that the image-flash acts as its own 'anti-particle' so to speak and cancels itself out to allow me a short, less anxious few seconds to complete the check without a mini panic-attack triggering a scan restart. Although it worked a couple of times on this occasion, it is no guarantee I will be successful the next time, as *it depends entirely on the threshold of my anxiety being low enough to allow it*.

If you are able to complete a compulsion at the fourth attempt instead of the eighth, for example, you have *halved the time* wasted tormenting yourself and inevitably raising your anxiety above the manageable threshold. After just a week you will have freed-up hours of time to be better spent employing your energies in positive creative ways, reinforcing your increasing desire to be optimistic at beating the infernal compulsions.

Realise and relish, that by not wasting your time and energy with compulsions, you have now opened-up time to engage in pleasurable pursuits, as I call them. Doing something you enjoy diverts your worrying mind away from the demands of the OCD. You have created a double benefit for yourself by exchanging unnecessary, worrying torment for a necessary, enjoyable and beneficial time.

During the writing of this book, I thought that some of the content would probably be something I would be too embarrassed to reveal and finally publish because of the personal details of the warts'n'all descriptions, particularly the skin picking (page 51). But I gradually became convinced that I wanted my children to know why I was strange and difficult to live with. If they bother to read this book at all, and with part of a lifetime's experience behind them, perhaps they will begin to understand and forgive.

Over the years, I have been moved by others' stories of their experiences and battle with OCD, depression and addiction to tranquillisers and antidepressants - now I can share mine with this book.

A significant part of my story is missing and a few know why. Events unknown to me at the time took place during the years approximately between 1972 and 1977.

Richard E Harding, August 2016

CHAPTER ONE

ISOLATION

The ominous phrase below the embryo-foetus image on the title page is the description I gave to a psychotherapist to explain how I felt during four years of bedridden isolation and total despair from 1996 until 2000. The precise wording was: 'a blackened embryo in a cotton coffin' to describe the curled-up hopelessness of my useless blackened (as in burnt-out) body awaiting death or recovery. My mind was in a state of suspended animation or limbo because I was helpless and hopeless and at a dead-end, hoping to die each and every night. I remember little of this time and so I cannot elaborate on the days, months and finally years and how I coped - I just mentally switched off.

Virtually ignored by my wife and children living in the same big house, an old converted church, I had to endure my inability to look after myself during a complete nervous breakdown caused by severe obsessive compulsive disorder, addiction to lorazepam (Ativan) tranquilliser, suicidal depression and a recent additional heart attack and arrhythmia. Unbeknown to me at this time, my massive heart attack in the late 1980s had left my heart severely weakened, producing extensive scar tissue of my left ventricle muscle which resulted in adverse electrical activity causing episodes of irregular fast heartbeat and greatly reduced blood flow with low oxygen levels.

The doctor who called at my home at that time had insisted I only had indigestion and it was an hour before an ambulance was finally called, resulting in untold heart damage due to the delay. I will never forgive him.

I had been addicted to a high dose of lorazepam after my family doctor gave me the medication to help me overcome severe anxiety and OCD in the early 1980s to supposedly enable me to finish my full-time science degree at a Cambridge college - my home town.

My personality changed as I became irritable, obnoxious and intolerant as a result of this mind-altering drug - and the OCD became worse, not better. *(See Appendix page 147)*

I later discovered this drug should only be prescribed for up to ten days. *So, my family doctors had double-crippled my life* it seems, and, after an immense struggle finishing my third year at college, resulting in another nervous breakdown, I was no longer able to work and my marriage was breaking up. *My degree was for nothing.*

Trying to cut down on the lorazepam proved fruitless and I remained on this terrible drug for a total of twenty years by the time I finally stopped the benzodiazepines by gradually tapering off with diazepam (Valium), a weaker version of this drug group. I took my last half low-dose tablet after our divorce in September 2001 after I had moved to Norfolk. Since 1996, my wife, most of my children and so-called friends have had nothing to do with me. I continue to find this bizarre.

After this 1996 nervous breakdown my life existed alone in my room for four years. I managed to get to the toilet for defaecation, but used plastic bottles in the bedroom for urination because regular trips to the toilet became impossible. My wife came in briefly once a day with a tray of food and drink and to empty my urine bottles, but she would never stay to speak with me, despite my pleadings every day.

Over the course of months I developed a nervous stutter in my anxious, desperate and futile attempts trying to speak with her before she went out of the room. My children didn't ever come to see me or even call through the door. The bedroom curtains were left permanently half-closed because I couldn't open or close them daily. As a consequence my only view of the outside world was of a tall tree in the middle-distance, visible above an ivy-covered brick wall. In the winter months I could see crows on the branches of this tree and had a game with myself over the years to count the maximum number of crows at any one time. Even this innocent pastime presented me with its own anxiety problem because the narrow gap between the curtains only allowed me to see one side of the tree at a time, causing me to move my head to see and count any additional crows on the other side. How could I ever be sure of the total number on the tree simultaneously? The crow counting was all I could do. I was totally unable to deal with putting on music or a TV, nor could I read. All the time was spent curled up like an embryo in my cotton coffin - alone with my agonising, tormenting thoughts, dreams and nightmares.

I remember nothing about all those lost years, except that I was constantly aware of not knowing why I was left like this by everyone. No one called a doctor or indeed anyone to help me.

When the year 2000 rolled around, someone told me that I was to have help at the Maudsley-Bethlem hospital in

Beckenham, Kent. My wife and daughter came with me to the hospital where I was diagnosed with what I already knew: OCD.

After many weeks receiving cognitive behavioural and exposure therapy at the hospital and with regular visits home, I was making good progress by eliminating some of my compulsions. *This made me feel there was definite hope to enable me to start a new life out of my bed*. I spent many hours with my fellow inmates trying to help them overcome their problems with no success. My wife refused to speak to my psychotherapist on the phone and upon my return home only answered anything I said in as few words as possible, always with a stony glare upon her face. I still don't know why I was treated like this after making such promising progress – it was as if I no longer existed!

On one of my previous visits home, my wife had told me that I was no longer in charge of the house or my family and that it was like I had returned from the dead, and that I was ugly and evil. Most of the children followed suit and ignored me as I spent the next year again on my own, mainly in my bedroom, that same eternal room, but this time I was able to function reasonably well and could play music, write and type up the verses and go out of the house. The important thing I was told at the hospital was to have support at home. I had none. No-one would discuss or even make mention of my plight or my successes. I gradually slipped back into the obsessive-compulsive cycle, but all the while aware that I must not let myself be broken by my uncaring family and end up bedridden again.

After our divorce I lived alone for the first time in my life in a cosy, detached, two-bed bungalow in Norfolk; however, I was a recluse and riddled with worsening OCD. After a couple of years I decided I would make the bold step to move to France and bought a house in need of repair. I sold my car for a deposit on the property and prepared to move to Central France.

It was a week to go when I had another heart attack, resulting in hospitalisation in King's Lynn with procedures performed at Papworth hospital, including the fitting of a pacemaker-defibrillator. Whilst in hospital my bungalow went to the new owner and all my belongings were packed up and taken to my French home by one of my elder sons and his girlfriend. *Matthew and Louise became the only people to care and help me.*

Alone, and with worsening heart problems and barely manageable OCD, I boiled in the summer and froze in the winter, unable to cut and move wood for my stove. The house needed work I now couldn't possibly achieve and each winter for three successive years, when I was out of bed, I sat ensconced in layers of clothes over my pyjamas with an overcoat and scarf directly in front of a glowing bottled-gas fire with only my two cats to preserve my failing sanity until the warm spring arrived. Endless times.

The great problem with OCD is that its dark shadow of depression is never far away. My remote and isolated existence would quickly give way to deep depression. Awake in my bed one day I saw streams of thin, black, shiny entities moving along the join between the ceiling and the wall. They moved to the corner near the window and collected there. More of these black, shiny, crack-dwellers moved along the top of the wall around the room at speed.

These tentacles from hell were one very weird hallucination. Looking down beside my bed at my bag, they were there too, running along the seams to collect in the corners. Averting my glance, they were still there when I looked again, reinforcing my belief they were real.

Later, downstairs, they were on my computer, running along the join between the screen and the frame. I honestly thought I was witnessing the activity of static electricity which naturally collect at the screen edges and in the corners of cathode ray tubes of old-style monitors and TVs. To my mind the static charge was manifesting itself, allowing me to see it. I felt excited and looked forward to telling others that I had actually seen it! I didn't see it ever again. I was quite disappointed but at the same time relieved.

Another time I believed my wife and children had died in a ferry accident. They had been exploring an out-of-bounds lower deck some time after the ship had docked, and this particular design of ship flooded this special maintenance deck to lower the ship in the water for some reason. They were trapped by the water flooding in and had all drowned. I cried bitterly for four hours sitting alone in my kitchen, totally believing this imagined situation to be true. I was in a terrible state of utter despair and thought my adjoining French neighbours may have heard me, but nobody called to see if I was all right – the story of my life. I had to telephone my son Matthew in England for him to convince me it *was* all imagined. Unfortunately, I was unable to grasp the French language and so suffered isolation from my French neighbours.

Having lived in France for three-and-a-half years my deteriorating health prompted my return to England, despite not being able to sell my French house. I no longer qualified for medical treatment in France so I quickly established contact with the NHS and went to live with someone I had sincerely believed to be a good, caring friend – how wrong I was. I suffered gross anxiety and several more nervous breakdowns over two years as a result of this control freak's mental abuse, but miraculously hung on to my control of the OCD. I used to record little videos of my despair on my cell phone, face distorted by anguish and tears.

At one time I just walked out, and with Matthew and Louise's help packed all my belongings into an old small car I bought off the street and bought a small tent from a Canterbury outdoor pursuits shop. My plan was to live in a field rather than deteriorate any more in that hostile environment. I booked a few weeks at a camp site near Margate, even though I was still weak from another of the many heart operations I had over the months. I had no plans what to do from there - all I knew was that I had to get away from that shared flat purely as a survival instinct. I was in daily phone contact with Matthew back in Cambridgeshire.

I spent those May days in constant discomfort, not being able to stand up in the small tent. I only had my mobile phone, biscuits, kitchen-roll tissues, wet-wipes and a bottle of water with me in the tent. I had to endure severe bouts of claustrophobia and temperature changes between very cold and very hot. In the evenings I went into the village for a meal at the local pub - I dislike pubs, but the people there were friendly and helpful. Even though I am a scientist and atheist, I gained strength from the ambience inside the big stone village church and even verbally asked for help.

One day I had to call for an ambulance because of returning chest pains and was taken to Margate hospital where I remained for a few days. I explained to them about my tent situation in the hope that they might be able to arrange for temporary alternative accommodation, but to no avail. I continued to live in a bigger tent near to Matthew in

Cambridgeshire for a few weeks and then in his garden shed.

I decided the only thing to do was to return to my French house, so I packed up all the things I had brought over with me and drove half-way across France back to my house one Saturday and into Sunday. The journey took me about ten hours and was horrendous. I became disorientated and lost and spent the night trying to sleep in the driving seat at a remote service station.

The next day I eventually arrived at my house and spent most of the week in bed exhausted, ill and very depressed. I could no longer claim for medical expenses in France and realised I was in a mess, so the very next Saturday I drove all the way back to England; thank goodness I hadn't had the strength to unpack my car. The journey back was much better as there are Calais ferry signs quite soon after being on the main road north, nevertheless, I don't know how I made it back feeling so ill with worrying chest pains – I just had to keep going in survival mode again. I was forced to return to that nightmare shared flat and started looking for another room.

Remaining in south east England, I eventually moved to a room in the next town where I only had use of a small room, mainly taken up by the bed, a large wardrobe and an armchair. Again, I was from the frying pan into a new fire. The street outside had a gang of young feral youths who congregated outside the house under a large tree every day (my room was downstairs at the front), shouting, swearing, drinking, spitting and moving in and out of the front gardens; it drove me dangerously close to yet another complete breakdown. I was constantly worried my car would be vandalised because I'd already seen the rear wiper pulled and forced myself to peer through a carefully constructed corner of the net curtains in an uncomfortable twisted position for hours on end to avoid detection. The room above me was occupied by an excessively noisy woman, with sudden bangs and loud thuds on the ceiling jolting my delicate senses. Six people occupied this semi-detached house.

On the brink of suicide, I attended a clinic where I spoke to people who offered no solution whatsoever as I constantly shook violently with hopeless, uncontrollable anxiety. I thought I would be hospitalised because I made it clear I was contemplating and planning suicide by jumping from the top of a nearby block of flats. *It seems that to be taken seriously with talk of ending your own life, you have to have seriously attempted it. That is why so many people end their misery.*

I had been given an emergency telephone number in case I felt I could no longer cope and was a danger to myself, *despite already making it clear that was already the case*. I called the number that evening and two young women arrived to speak with me in my room. I proceeded to explain my hopeless situation, all the time visibly shaking and speaking in a cracked-up voice, hardly able to control my emotions. After the best part of an hour they left, saying to call again if I was in trouble.

Why didn't they understand I WAS in trouble and in dire need of a solution to avert my almost imminent suicide. What was to follow saved my life.

I scoured the Internet looking for rooms in or near to Cambridge, my home town, to which I longed to return, having wished I had never left. I called an old friend to ask if I could stay for a few days whilst I investigated some addresses of rooms I had found advertised on the Internet. It was to prove fruitless: one had been let and another failed to answer my call. I was desperate, and was to return to my planned demise the next day when my friend's girlfriend suggested I went to get a newspaper to check out the ads for rooms. I pointed out that it was hopeless to expect any result as it was already evening, but she insisted I went along to the shop with her to get a few things and to buy a paper.

There was only one little advertisement on the relevant page: a room to rent with a phone number. This thoughtful woman dialled the number on her mobile phone and handed it to me to speak. To my surprise we arranged to call at the address that evening! This meeting with my prospective landlord, David, resulted in saving my life.

I returned to that life-draining room in the south-east of England, and a week or so later Matthew and Louise arrived to help me pack and move back to Cambridge. Four years later I am still here - writing this.

Update 2015:

After another brief move to a landlady artist into a bigger room, I was finally offered a housing society bungalow in the countryside in March 2014, where I cope much better with my anxiety; but sadly my heart condition is worsening leaving me increasingly unable to do anything much physically. I continue to write and have now finished my third book: The Halloween Chamber (May 2016). David has remained my friend.

CHAPTER TWO

CHILDHOOD

Had I been able to choose to be born into this world, knowing how it would be, I would have declined. I had spent my childhood as an only child to a nervous, tearful mother. Why she felt she had to tell her young child about the pain I put her through at childbirth and that I was supposed to be a girl, Janet, I don't know! She was constantly anxious and crying and had compulsions I noticed as a young child. She was to become agoraphobic, with my poor father having to do everything in the house as well as hold down his job as a laboratory technician. The time was the late forties and I was born mid-day on October 31st 1946 – Halloween!

I cannot recall any love, cuddles or affection from either parent and in retrospect I understand that I was unwanted.

I soon developed compulsions of my own: I kept my books and my toys pristine, hardly daring to open or even handle them; especially the books for fear of damaging them by tearing or creasing the pages. Apart from the quarter mile walk to school during my younger years, I was not allowed far from the house most of the time because my mother feared I would drown in the nearby river. Her 'nerves', as she called them, prevented other children being invited into the house.

I was terrified by the noisy dustmen banging the metal lids on the metal dustbins at the back of our house underneath my window. At this time, in the late forties and early fifties, the dustmen came through the back gate and into the garden to collect the bins. The coal-men delivering sacks of coal into our coal shed were very distressing too – I vividly remember the roaring, rushing sound of the coal being poured from the sacks into the small, bricked space; to this day I am very disturbed by the sound of the dustcart and the plastic bins banging and being noisily wheeled about.

One of my first childhood memories was of a holiday taken at Sheringham on the north Norfolk coast in about 1950; we travelled up from Cambridge by steam train (I believe it still was steam-driven at that time). We stayed at a private house, and when we arrived I was given toys to play with belonging to the host's little girl. I distinctly remember playing nervously on the floor near to an armchair one of my parents was sitting on, when the little girl came into the room. I hid my head beneath the armchair frozen with terror because I felt so guilty playing with her toys. I remember it as my first emotion.

So, I had no friends and no birthday parties and spent my later, lonely childhood roaming Grantchester Meadows; we lived right next to them in Newnham, west Cambridge. I remember feeling at one with nature, especially during those long summer months alone: the gentle, breeze-swayed meadow grass hosting myriad busy insects and the magical trickling streams with their dragonflies, frogs, tadpoles and sticklebacks; the wheeling skylarks calling from high in the blue, cloud-billowed sky, and the lazy river Cam with its enigmatic trailing willow branches reflected in its shadowed surface. The early Pink Floyd's song, *Grantchester Meadows* reminds me so much of those days. David Gilmour lived just around the corner I later discovered!

I felt as if I existed inside a bubble - a sort of transparent, thin membrane which separated me from total reality, and one which I had expected to burst, to at last put me in the real world of people from which I distinctly felt apart. It never happened and I remained within that part-reality-defying membrane for most of my life.

Recently, with lower anxiety, I have at last found relative peace, and feel much freed from the restraints of unreality, especially as I realised many years ago that I probably had Asperger's Syndrome (AS). OCD and depression are strong comorbid partners of AS and autism, but *I am unsure that AS is actually a part of the autistic spectrum.*

I believe the AS type is an evolution-driven trade-off: enhanced intelligence with the ability for intense analytical study of detail and examination of systems, traded for social awareness, along with its trivia and small-talk nonsense.

I believe my late mother was mildly AS with OCD tendencies, and also her brother and father. Having Asperger's Syndrome is not a bad thing. In fact I would not change it, because it allows me deep insight into reality - not people-reality, but into the realms of complicated science subjects which have become my all-consuming passion. My science degree in biology and geology led inexorably to a deep interest in subjects we didn't touch on: namely cosmology - the physics of the gargantuan immensity of the universe, and the infinitesimal, mysterious world of quantum mechanics.

During my childhood, I seem to have been an increasingly disturbed child. As a very young child I was bullied by my neighbour's son of the same age and then by a boy who hit me and a teacher who punched me at my junior school which had a profound effect upon my view of other people. The bullying carried on at my senior school and my first job. I suppose my Asperger's disposition is a target for neurotypicals who see it as a weakness.

At the age of eleven or twelve I attended a private school in west Cambridge. I succeeded in science subjects and loved every minute of the biology, algebra, geometry and physics lessons, whilst most of my male classmates were only interested in socialising.

In class, I had a writing problem with repeating full stops on the same spot until they came through the paper. We had metal-nibbed ink-dip pens with wooden handles and white ceramic inkwells popped into holes at the end of the pen and pencil troughs in the corner of the graffiti-scarred wooden desks, and purple blotting paper at that time in the early sixties! My always tidy desk was 'stirred up' on many occasions, and I hated swapping a test answer page to be marked by others, because I *knew* the answers were all correct and expected ten out of ten *every* time, and if they weren't I questioned the others' marking ability. I was a pompous know-all nerd! I remember being so proud of my father for being a scientist that I used to boast about him.

I had no part in any social life or sport, whilst my classmates were all living normal lives. I loved these subjects about the reality of the scientifically explained world, not the frivolous out-and-about meanderings of so-called normal people. To me, they were showing little interest in what really mattered: *How the world and its things worked.*

An older boy of about fourteen spoke to me in the playground; he wanted me to see a raft he had built beside the river. I was keen on rafts and stuff like that, so pedalled off on my bike after school to meet him in woodland on the river bank. When I arrived, all seemed rather mysterious with this boy half hidden in the bushes and talking to me. He was naked holding his erect penis and asked me to touch it and then to lower him into the water! The raft did not exist and I remember being terrified and running for my bike to pedal away.

In retrospect, this was probably not too out of the ordinary an event to happen with adolescent boys at senior school. But I had not long left junior school and didn't know what was happening, just that it was some kind of weird, scary behaviour I didn't understand.

This event had such a profound effect on me that I remained guilt-ridden, anxious and terrified for the rest of my school-days and beyond.

I felt some awful burden of guilt was upon me, that I had done something terrible that others must not find out had happened. The fact I had done nothing but be an observer of a boy discovering sex did nothing to ease my despairing feeling of guilt and gross debilitating anxiety. I told no-one.

I believe this single event may have been responsible for propelling me into full-blown OCD. Anxiety-driven torment.

CHAPTER THREE

MY FIRST JOB

With my six GCE 'O' levels I followed in my father's footsteps into bacteriology. It was a big mistake. I worked as a junior laboratory assistant at the Cambridge University School of Veterinary Medicine's clinical pathology laboratory. Here, I was bullied by two people: the veterinary surgeon head of the department who menacingly stood behind me watching what I was doing at the bench and taking every opportunity to suggest I had my hair cut, and a woman haematology worker who kept nagging me to fill the distilled water bottles when I was obviously busy and she was not. On one occasion she pulled out the stool from under me whilst I was working with bacteria at my bench, because I told her to do it herself; this resulted in a reprimand from my hair-obsessed boss. Bacteriology is most definitely something an OCDer should never contemplate - but I didn't know that at the time. I didn't know what this *unreal world* thing which afflicted me was all about - no one did!

The condition and odd behaviour we now know as OCD was described centuries ago and mainly associated with scrupulosity and moral perfection. The autistic personality has been recognised for over a hundred years, but in 1963, when I was seventeen, it was virtually unknown outside of psychiatry. (Verses: '1964' page 169)

I was aware of feeling distinctly odd and being so different to everyone else: being increasingly preoccupied with neatness, order, perfection, cleanliness, fear, doubt and hesitation, and with a persistent sort of 'rap' talking in my head. Working in a laboratory is the last place on Earth an obsessive-compulsive person should be let loose in – especially one with benches laden with bacteria; it took its toll early on with hand washing. Needing to have a pee was a marathon event, with me being absent from the laboratory for inordinately long periods of time and privately stricken with an uncontrollable fear of infection.

After leaving it as long as I could, it started with me washing my hands in the dirty laboratory sink and having to wipe my hands on the green towel used by others. Then it was off to the general toilets frequented by veterinary students just back from sticking their arms up cow's bottoms. They left the sinks smelly and dirty with farm mud and god knows what else from the often diseased animals. I was terrified with obsessional fear, unable to cope physically and mentally with the compulsion to stand at the sink washing over and over again under running water, with people in and out continually.

I had to wash my hands such that I was convinced, as far as possible, that I would avoid transferring any germs to my penis when I finally allowed myself the bliss of emptying my aching bladder. Even the act of urination was riven with fear and doubt that I would touch my penis or hands on the dirty off-white porcelain urinal wall which would ensure I caught the dreaded lurgi - *the most feared of all known diseases!*

Many times my *nice* boss would come looking for me; he knew where I would be. Of course I couldn't just say: "Sorry about that, I have an unreasonable compulsion to continue washing my hands for far too long in case I get the dreaded lurgi." Or: "Sorry, I have unheard-of OCD!" It was assumed that I suffered constipation and had remedies suggested to me as a consequence!

This was the first time I remember having the compulsion to ensure my trouser fly zip was fully closed; I would count the zip transits and have to finish with the zip up on four – it also had to *feel right*. In addition, I would feel compelled to recheck it later, inevitably restarting the ritual. Still, today, at the age of sixty nine, this counting up-down zip compulsion has remained with me – utterly crazy!

As a naïve youngster at this veterinary hospital's clinical pathology lab in 1963, I wasn't prepared for the horror of the post-mortem room. As part of my job at the laboratory I was required to help out my boss in this evil room. I can only describe it as a living nightmare – a blood-fest scene of horror.

Animals were routinely killed in this room: a very large white-tiled room with a floor designed to channel away vast quantities of blood and swilling water into a central drain. The man in charge of this killing floor was an abnormally jovial, tall, large man called Jack, who regularly despatched pigs, sheep, cows and horses among other animals. They were stunned by a hefty electric charge administered by electrode pads on tongs whilst being restrained in galvanised steel metal pens.

On one particular occasion a cow or bull was to be killed and I was not forewarned as to what was to follow. I watched as the beast was first stunned and then, on the floor, had its skull punctured by an explosive captive bolt gun in an horrific shuddering episode which was truly terrifying for me. After the metal bolt had impaled itself and was removed, the big post-mortem man took a long piece of sturdy twisted wire and proceeded to poke, stab and rootle it in the hole to mash the poor creature's brain. I vividly remember the convulsions and twitchings. Then the hot, sweating animal's throat was cut.

My job was to pass large, 250 ml sterile bottles to my boss, who collected the spurting blood from the neck wound and returned them to me dripping red wet. This was repeated as quickly as possible whilst the blood was flowing - probably dozens of bottles were filled in around ten minutes. I helped to freeze-dry the blood in the bottles to be reconstituted when needed for bacterial growth media production in the media kitchen, in the days before media was bought pre-prepared.

We were red with the dying essence of this noble animal and I really don't know if I ever recovered. I later learned that meat cuts were distributed to various workers in the unit, but I refused - the remains later fed into the incinerator in the next room. That horror was not the last I would experience.

On the occasions when Jack, the post-mortem man, was away on holiday or through illness, it was required for my (nice) boss and I to man the incinerator by loading it with collected animal parts and to light the fearsome gas furnace. I was not prepared for helping to lift a whole horse's head with open eyes through the iron hatch - very heavy and scary! These animals were usually those used in experiments which were no longer required as they couldn't be used again because they had to be fresh and healthy before the experiment started.

I loved the small animals in the animal house when I visited to see them - the white mice, rabbits, dogs and cats.

I was later to witness my boss injecting a white rabbit directly into its heart with barbiturate or something similar to stop it beating - its reward for staying alive during a test to see if a particular bacterial organism would grow within its innocent body. It was my job to crucify its lifeless body to a wooden board in the laboratory and to proceed with a post-mortem examination of its internal organs and take samples for my bacteriological investigation - one of the jobs I was learning. Lovely creatures were tortured and killed just so some vet could give the right antibiotic to a dog lovers' dog! *Why did I allow myself to be a part of this?*

Another laboratory job for my OCD-ridden mind to cope with was parasitology. I had to take mainly dog, sheep, pigs or horse faeces and mix it using a metal spatula in a small white bowl containing a strong saline solution to enable any parasite eggs present to float to the surface to then be extracted by pipette and examined under the microscope in a special graticuled counting chamber. I had to mix the vile fluid whilst keeping my lips held tightly shut and my head half-turned away to avoid accidentally ingesting the microscopic eggs from a splash. The two kinds of parasite eggs I remember looking for were *Toxocara canis* in dogs and *Fasciola hepatica* in sheep and pigs. I was told that the workers in the main parasitology department expected worm infestation as part of the job!

My main job at this veterinary hospital was bacteriology, and this involved isolating and identifying different types of pathogenic bacteria from various animal sources such as faeces, urine, sputum, pus and diseased tissue from post-mortems (such as my white rabbit). Many of the samples came in from outside veterinary surgeons in Cambridge and the Equine Research Station at Newmarket, and so samples could be from pet mice, birds, rats, hamsters, guinea pigs, cats, dogs, sheep, pigs and horses. However, some animals were big exotic creatures from a circus including giraffes, lions and tigers which were examined and treated inside a large round building called The Rotunda, because of its shape, and mainly used for Newmarket race horses.

The bacterial colonies are grown on special media, usually blood agar, in flat, round Petri dishes, incubated at 37°C and examined the next day. I had all sorts of nasty bugs to deal with including Salmonella, TB, Anthrax, Staphylococcus aureus, Streptococcus and Eschericia coli. I sat at the laboratory bench slaving over a hot Bunsen, holding open Petri dishes to closely examine the scores of colonies, each of which contained tens of thousands of potentially lethal organisms. I had this obsessional fear of flicking my tongue out and quickly licking them because I knew I could do this in a split second. Occasionally, I had to deal with mould growth in the dish, having been told of Aspergillus, a nasty mould which grows in the airways of victims in a plaque formation. Ringworm, a misnomer, is another fungal infection which I feared working with, being constantly aware that my hair could be infected and fall out! No health and safety measures then, and amazingly everyone smoked!

Excessive hand-washing became an essential part of the daily routine at this Laboratory From Hell, brought about by this perfectly understandable fear of those nasty pathogenic germs. It was a compulsion which added to my ever-growing repertoire of incapacitating OCD behaviour.

In retrospect, I wonder why I waited until I suffered a nervous breakdown before I had to leave that first job. I was a naïve teenager who had no parental guidance whatsoever.

This job was responsible for exacerbating my anxious disposition to the point where I was never able to cope properly with life again.

Enduring these first years at work was so hard for me, not only the hand-washing, but also checking became almost uncontrollable. I began remaining in the laboratory after everyone else had left for home. Those five rooms took on a sinister atmosphere that made being there alone a very uncomfortable experience, especially in the winter-time and early darkness checking for dead bodies under the benches.

After finishing my work and hindered by OC slowness, hesitation and repeated checking through doubt, I would embark on checking each room - even those I had not occupied during the day. There were numerous gas taps I felt compelled to check to ensure they were definitely *off*. It wasn't good enough to visually check them, I had to physically ensure their off position. Removing my fingers and hand were an additional trial because I was never sure that I hadn't accidentally knocked a tap *slightly on*. If the tap didn't look absolutely at right-angles to the spout I would have to push the accursed yellow plastic lever once more. Many gas taps were *not* at right-angles at the stop position, due to poor manufacturing tolerances or wear, but I was able to memorise which taps were affected and so avoid wasting time trying to adjust them. Typically, each room had six double gas taps. My obsession was that if any taps were actually leaking gas, then it would be *my* fault if there was a fire or explosion. Each room could take a half hour or more before I could *feel* it was all right to leave it. If I was interrupted by a cleaner I would have to leave the room to return when the cleaner had moved on. This meant starting all over again until I was satisfied to continue with the next room further down the corridor.

Not only were there gas taps I was compelled to check, but also water taps and electrical plugs and switches. I had to push the wall plugs to ensure they were all the way in and that they were on or off as required. Incubators would be on all the time to grow the bacteria and so I would have to check they were definitely switched on by the appliance indicator light *and* the switch lever at the plug in the down position.

The hours of intense staring hurt my eyes, and after a prolonged period I could no longer believe my tired, stinging, often watering eyes. If I needed the toilet during this procedure, despair would be overwhelming, because I then had all the washing ritual to overcome, knowing I had to return to the never-ending task of checking the rooms.

The embarrassment of repeatedly meeting the cleaner and having to think of something convincing to say every night was something I didn't need. "Working late again are we?" became the expected response to our encounters.

If I needed to defaecate at work, the prospect of sitting down on a filthy toilet was terrifying in the extreme. The thought that my penis would inevitably touch inside the porcelain bowl was minimised by numerous sheets of toilet paper carefully arranged over the area and the seat for me to precariously sit on. Then I had the wiping ritual and the floor check to endure as a finalé.

After maybe an hour or two, I would finally be satisfied I had checked all the rooms and experience the wonderful relief at having finished all the rituals wash over me, and then to feel the fresh evening air waft into my nostrils as I unlocked my bicycle to pedal home exhausted, both physically and mentally, all the while terrified I would doubt one of the dozens of actions previously undertaken and have to return to check it without the intense compulsion to have to again check everything else. Thankfully, I didn't ever have to put myself through that additional torment – I guess I'd had enough by then!

Once home I would eat, wash my hair and get round to my girlfriend's house at some unreasonable hour - usually gone eight, with an excuse of working late. Yes, amazingly I had a girlfriend, whom I married when I was twenty and she nineteen. Then it all went horribly wrong.

I suffered a nervous breakdown so profound that I was unable to continue my life doing anything worthwhile.

Trying to get up out of bed, wash and dress became a nightmare of compulsive rituals and gross anxiety I had no control over. It was 1967, we were just married and living in a flat in a nice area of north Cambridge near to both our parents. Compulsive hand-washing had become so bad that on one occasion I washed continually at the bathroom sink for six hours, leaving my hands dry and white.

One day, putting my legs into my trousers just didn't *feel right* and I burst into tears with my new wife beside me. I couldn't make it to the laboratory that day, nor for months afterwards. I remained bedridden whilst my young, patient wife continued her secretarial work and paid the rent. I am so lucky she stayed with me, but she had to witness and endure the grip this unknown affliction was having on me and our relationship. Often, my bewildered mother called with a hot meal for me during the day; that was lovely!

A mental health worker called to speak with me, and it was suggested that I spent some time in hospital to try and sort things out. I remember thinking I was so normal compared to others in my psychiatric ward, and I was soon home again. I couldn't bear to go back to the laboratory and I was offered a job in the laboratory workshop putting up shelves and fixing windows. I felt humiliated doing this comparatively menial work and the OCD again became intolerable. I remember being claustrophobically mentally 'stuck' in a cupboard under the stairs where I was putting up shelves in the restrictive space and suffering a panic attack – a crashing nervous onslaught.

Even though I had a hellish time in my first job at the animal hospital laboratory, it was an exciting time of cultural change in the form of music, mainly by The Beatles and The Rolling Stones. Longer hair and the hippy culture gave people, including me, a diversion from their daily mundanity.

One of my greatest loves was to go into town to buy the latest vinyl music album by my favourite band; but handling it when I had opened the wonderful, colourful cardboard packaging at home ruined the excitement. Part of me wanted to enjoy the thrill of putting the vinyl record on the turntable and hearing the songs whilst studying every detail of the printed cover. (Remember, this was before cassettes, CDs and streaming digital music and stored files accessed on computers, iPods, tablets and smart-phones!) The anxious OCD part of me, demanded I check the surfaces for any scratches by adjusting a light source to sweep highlights over the pristine jet-black surface by altering its angle, all the while holding the disc by its edges – of course! Then, to be finally terrified I might scratch the surface myself by somehow knocking the needle in my adrenalised anxious state, constantly checking the tiny needle's contact with the recording surface, unable to take my eyes away for fear of pulling it away.

I have since realised this is my first memory of the dreaded 'eye-strings' which would continue to plague my life to the present day.

Thankfully, I had a good social life in Cambridge, centred at the river bridge next to The Mill public house and Laundress Green in about 1965, which helped offset my OCD misery. I met up with some people whom I had overheard in The Anchor pub were starting a guitar group. I joined and we practiced and played for a year or two at various venues and I had a great time. Sadly, some band members didn't get along and the group disbanded.

I think that loss of exciting, active socialising may have eventually contributed to my headlong decent into full-blown OCD and my inability to work after this first nervous breakdown soon after I married.

It was seven years until I worked again, this time selling tents at a garden centre. I told the guy I worked with about my obsessional problems and he was kind and understanding and we got along fine (Thanks, Baz!). Because I no longer had to hide my odd behaviour I was more relaxed and the obsessions and compulsions became less and more manageable. The worst compulsions for me at that time were checking the car was locked with all the lights off and the windows shut and the toilet rituals.

The car checking ritual could take up most of the evening after I arrived home and could involve my wife to check for me when I couldn't carry on through exhaustion. I had to see she did it properly and would often ask her to repeat a particular check. She would eventually refuse to check at all.

CHAPTER FOUR

HOARDING, COLLEGE AND BENZOS

Around this time, from the 1970s onwards, I began collecting stuff and hoarding. The dining room became a pile of neatly stacked objects and boxes - possessions which I felt a desperate need to retain even at the expense of the dining room space. Very soon there would only remain a pathway for part of the way into the room. For me to go into this area was fraught with fear, because I didn't want to knock any of my carefully placed objects. I dreaded having to readjust and reposition their placement - necessary even to millimetre tolerances. I started collecting old typewriters thrown out by stores who replaced them for customers with word processor computers and printers.

I first noticed them piled-up outside these Cambridge shops and soon investigated around the delivery areas at the back to find more and more. I had great trouble lifting the heavy machines into my camper van and then into the house and *I think this straining and lifting may have contributed to my first heart attack.* Most of these typewriters ended up in the shed or the loft, and one or two electric golf-ball type models were used to type my handwritten science and book novel writings for the first time in the 1980s.

That first novel finally became Cryptic Visions, published in 2016, over thirty years later!

Rubbish skips were like treasure troves and I would bring wood and other useful looking stuff home with me – even bags of plastic coat hangers from outside clothes shops which we didn't need! The garden shed became full of the less precious things I couldn't throw away. The passageway to the back gate became blocked with all manner of items and could not be used. The loft was packed with items from my younger years I had brought with me, arranged with walkways to access the boxes. I always have great trouble in lofts and attics and find it difficult to leave everything to descend the ladder because it seems so final putting out the light and closing the trapdoor when I am never sure everything was finished up there, especially that the light was off – like most fridges. Lofts are surreal places for me: either too hot or too cold, cramped with splintery, head-height beams and a strange receiver for outside sounds doubled and amplified from the front and back of the house together through the gaps under the eaves in a bizarre sort of stereo.

In retrospect, I don't know how my wife and children put up with the mess in the house. *I'm sure these living conditions were the beginning of building resentment towards me which would prove to only increase with time.* Another obsession to develop was collecting meticulously executed VHS video cassette recordings of TV programs – particularly the *X-Files.* I ended-up with dozens of episodes, all labelled and coded and with the advertisements skillfully edited out. Other programs of interest were given the same treatment and I still have several large boxes of these video recordings in my shed which I have never watched since recording them. I cannot just throw them away. The X-Files American television series went on to develop a cult following, so perhaps I could sell them to a collector - or watch them again myself; I still own a player!

After a couple of years I changed my job from tent seller to become the manager of The Coffee Shop in Cambridge, selling coffee beans and grounds to the colleges, hotels, local restaurants, cafés and to the public. Two years or so of this was mind-numbing; I needed a job in which I could use my scientific knowledge. I applied for another laboratory job, feeling that I could now manage my OCD.

The job was with a retired professor running a cancer research department at Cambridge Addenbrooke's hospital. Professor Joseph Stanley Mitchell was the guy who pioneered radiotherapy at Cambridge in the early part of the last century. I had to learn to use an electron microscope and a photographic dark-room as well as prepare specimens. Although I was anxious because I was dealing with cancer cells, I enjoyed being able to work at my own pace.

As soon as I received the cancer cells from a colleague who had grown them in tissue culture, I exposed them to radiation and then killed them! Thankfully, I didn't have to worry too much that I may have been contaminated because I was able to cope with any fearful thoughts when they arose and successfully dismiss them.

During my time at the cancer research laboratory I studied for a biology diploma for one day and evening per week for two years; this involved zoology, botany, physics, chemistry and mathematics. I did very well with these favourite subjects of mine and I achieved a high pass mark. Because of this, I was offered a place in the full-time science degree course to eventually major in biology and geology. I mentioned this opportunity to my dear old professor and he wanted me to go ahead with it, to then return qualified and command a higher wage. This would be very welcome because I had several children to support. I think the year was 1979.

So it was I left the cancer research laboratory and took on a full-time college degree together with youngsters half my age; I had become that strange breed of mature student! The course was very intensive with a few young students dropping out and I felt proud I was able to cope with all the work and a home life with a wife, four children and the anxiety-ridden OCD. During those years at college the professor sadly died, shortly after his beloved wife's demise.

I passed all the subjects with good results in the first, and to a lesser extent, the second year, but the strain was getting to me. The OCD was gaining strength over me and I became increasingly aware that I was worrying what I had said to people, in case it was wrong, ambiguous or rude. The fact that I had *never* done this didn't provide the common-sense proof or assurance that I *never would*.

I would replay remembered conversations and put myself in the other person's position of hearing and interpreting what I had said in order to convince myself that nothing was offensive or ambiguous and that I had not made a fool of myself.

Also, I was unable to stop checking the classroom floors for any papers, pens or pencils I may have dropped, even though I am never in the habit of dropping things - I am always too neat and careful about how I go about things for that to happen. I am always aware of every little detail, however unimportant, continually over-tasking myself with the irrelevant trivia of going about things - whatever it is. Even things which should be accomplished automatically are analysed for errors and mistakes.

I cycled to and from college at one stage, and with my mind full of thoughts and images I needed to eliminate before I reached home, I would stop under an archway below residential flats and lean against the wall whilst still on my bicycle. I needed to replay and analyse all the accumulated *mental audio-video* of everything I had said and done during the busy college day to convince myself that all was well and that I hadn't upset anyone or done anything wrong. I desperately wanted a clear mind before I returned home to enable me to cope with family life in as normal a manner as possible. I rarely could manage this overwhelming task, often made all the more demanding by a nervous need to empty my bladder, so I would have to carry on the short distance home in the hope I could clear at least one of the accumulated worries, but I never could.

I am unable to filter out unimportant detail. I hang on to it to dissect it over and over again, just in case I have missed something important, because I reckon that this inevitably *will* happen at some time and I must remain resolutely vigilant.

In 1981, during the summer college break before the third and final year, I suffered another nervous breakdown and felt I couldn't carry on. I asked my doctor what I could do about my anxiety because I needed to finish the final year. The fool went on to prescribe me a high dosage of lorazepam (Ativan), the most powerful benzodiazepine tranquilliser, with no warnings or restrictions as to its use.

That prescription sealed the end of my career, my marriage and my relationship with my children and friends. My world fell apart.

This strong mood-altering tranquilliser offered me no benefit whatsoever. Yes, it changed my mood all right, to one of being obnoxious, intolerant, aggressive and hated.

I began behaving in a peculiar, uncaring manner to everyone, beyond the point where it was in any way acceptable. I felt myself go over the edge into some area of no return, like a person who has murdered and that it didn't matter if he killed again because it was too late - I had crossed the Rubicon.

It seemed as if I had let go and was behaving and speaking in all those ways I had dreaded and obsessed about previously. I suppose, in a way, it was some bizarre means to combat the OCD, by not caring what I said or did any more. I was tired and bedridden again and shouted at everyone over the smallest of issues.

I forced myself to finish that final year at college after a gap of a couple of years despite my anxiety and addiction to lorazepam, but at the presentation ceremony in 1985 it was all a big anticlimax – I felt no elation for my achievement and slid back into my crazy benzo world to endure my next nervous breakdown.

I was no longer able to get along with my wife, children, friends or anyone. I was gone.

CHAPTER FIVE

NAIL BITING AND SKIN PICKING

During the 1980s I suffered years of intense nail biting and skin picking. I would bite my fingernails all night long until it *felt right* to leave them – it never did. My shoulders, arms, hands and jaw would ache badly by the time I had finished a night session putting a strain on my heart; this happened almost every night. Many hours later with shredded nail-beds bleeding, I would apply tincture of iodine by running the fluid along the juncture line between the nail and skin. The resulting stinging was nothing short of utter bliss, providing the knowledge that I would avoid infection and that I had finished that night's compulsion at long last. Then I would sleep all day.

The skin picking was much worse: I would examine in minute detail the hair roots on my scrotum and proceed to squeeze, pick and gouge out the root bulbs with my barely existing fingernails. My body position to achieve this was agonising: sitting on the toilet, hunched over my drawn-up testicles and constantly wiping away the blood with acres of toilet tissue to enable me to see what I was doing. As with the nail biting, this would continue without a break for many hours until I was defeated by utter fatigue – it was pure hell! But that wasn't the end of it. For the next hour or so I would stand my exhausted body and aching back at the bathroom sink to embark on a tortuous hand and genital washing session. I believed the hair follicles were little warts and that I was going to infect myself with them popping-up all over my bitten nail beds and especially inside my foreskin. I imagine the fear of AIDs results in similar obsessive-compulsive genital cleaning behaviour.

The first stage of this arduous task was to turn on the tap with a tissue wad to protect the tap head from becoming infected with my imagined wart viruses and infected blood. I would then give my hands a preliminary thorough wash with just water until I felt they were clean enough to pick up the soap. Then, with a nail brush, I would scour my bitten nail beds for about half an hour whilst they bled.

The second stage of this procedure involved filling the sink with warm water and placing my testicles over the sink edge to facilitate the vigorous soaping of my scrotum with my hands. I dare not use a flannel at this stage for fear of contaminating it and having to discard it. The warm water made the bleeding continue and I washed until I could hardly remain standing. I then repeatedly washed my penis and inner thighs, as they *must* have also become contaminated. (*Contaminated* is a very scary word for us OCDers. My other non-germ contamination fears are wet paint, tiny broken glass fragments and molten candle wax and flame.)

The third stage was to stop the bleeding from the dozens of pick and gouge marks by dousing my scrotum with cold water until the bleeding became manageable. Then, armed with a copious supply of clean tissues, I patted the area dry. However, there always remained some small specks of blood and then seeping yellowish serum. Around an hour or two later I was able to put on clean underpants or my pyjamas to then collapse on the bed.

The picking could start up again even on the same day, or the very next time I went for a pee; I was just unable to prevent the urge to pick, despite knowing what hours of torture lay ahead of me.

As a spotty teenager living with my parents I picked my facial whiteheads and blackheads and first started on my scrotal hair follicles. The face ritual was manageable, but the scrotum picking late at night resulted in me running cold baths because I couldn't run the noisy gas geyser water-heater for fear of waking my parents across the landing because I would have been unable to explain myself. One freezing bath-full after another, I'd sit through the night and scrub my poor scrotum and hands raw. Often, by the time I had finished, cold, aching and exhausted, it would be only an hour or so before I needed to be at work at the laboratory and having to face another day of fear-inducing bacterial OCs and bullying.

My parents must have heard me during those nights of washing, but not once did they come to see what was wrong – Why?

Now on to 1994.

CHAPTER SIX

OUR CHURCH HOUSE

We moved house a few times and ended-up buying a derelict church in a Cambridgeshire village. We all lived in an old ex-seaside caravan in the graveyard after moving in the early hours of January 1st 1994, to remain there until the building renovation work was completed by November of that year. Four adults, four cats and two young children.

Outside, during each weekday, was a constantly noisy building site as workmen gradually transformed the ivy overgrown derelict church into what was supposed to be our dream home. I had drawn the plans for the whole church conversion before we moved on site. Then I suffered another heart attack, but survived despite having a severely damaged heart by now. When we finally moved out of the caravan ten months later and into the churchouse, we had the awesome task of decorating acres of walls and doors, including the large twenty foot high hall – the main part of this 1790s ex-United Reformed Church with its additional Victorian brick extensions. I was not up to the job.

Still dependant on lorazepam and with a weakened heart (I wasn't to know *how* weakened until many years later) I was struggling to stop the obsessions and compulsions. They finally overwhelmed me as we tried to get our church home into shape and my wife moved out of our bedroom.

A year later, in 1996, I became the dark embryo in that cotton coffin – my bed. No life, family, career or hope - just ignored. Why?

The times when I ventured out to the toilet to defaecate, I would stand behind my bedroom door, unable to open it. A tremendous effort was needed to open up into that alien space beyond my door. If I sensed or saw anyone in the large hall through the small gap in my partly opened door I would obsess over whether they saw me; I feared they would think I was spying on them.

My appearance must have been formidable: very long, lank, greasy hair and an overgrown moustache and beard – I was Rasputinesque.

When I felt the time was right, amidst an enormous panic attack, I would make a run for the stairs and up to the bathroom through the hall. There, I could relieve myself, together with all the attendant wiping and washing of hands rituals. The same surveillance procedure through the partially opened door took place before I returned downstairs to my room, with little thought of relief that another session was over, but instead, the dreaded thought of having to do this all over again in a few days time.

My wife continued her utter indifference to my plight and still had the fixed stony stare whenever our eyes met. The children seemed to be following their mother's example by virtually ignoring me on the rare occasions we met in the hall or on the stairs.

To this day I don't know why!

During the year following my return from Maudsley-Bethlem hospital from late 2000 - 2001 we decided to divorce, and were able to eventually sell our church and move out our separate ways. We divorced soon after the move. Most of my hoarded items found their final resting place at the local tip because there was just too much to take with me. It was a grim time, but I was able to not dwell on the loss of my things because I suppose I knew they would have to go sometime, so it was a kind of relief. On the day of the move, two vans arrived - one for me to go to my recently acquired Norfolk bungalow and one for the family I loved to move up the road to a big house in the village. The parting was surreal - no emotion, little talking.

OCD DREAMS

Enduring an OCD dream is terrifying. Checking is the biggest problem, which becomes a circular self-feeding process, building to a crescendo of hopelessness within the dream. Weird dreamscape scenarios are generated from past memories of disturbing experiences. Familiar places become distorted into terrifying dark places energised with the power to dispense adrenalised fear to me whilst I sleep.

This is the stuff of dreams, but amplified by obsessional thoughts, images and memories of past obsessive thoughts and compulsions, becomes the stuff of nightmares.

These often grotesque dreams and nightmares haunt my sleeping hours. Most nights I endure one or the other or multiples of both. The only escape is the need for me to empty my bladder. Even then, once up and standing dazed at the pedestal, it requires an enormous amount of mental effort to gradually make the distinction between what is real and what is the fantasy of the dream. This required mental effort to return to reality is difficult to summon at first, as this facility is badly depleted by the needs of the still partially active dream. Then it is back to bed dreading the next few hours of what my troubled, anxious mind will generate to torment me again.

I often experience hallucinations:

Recently, I have suddenly woken in bed and opened my eyes to see a staring unknown face right next to mine, a different, unrecognisable face each time; spiders on the wall; various large mosquitos and unknown hovering solid objects. I brushed away an unusual cream-coloured lizard from my duvet and have had two visions of complete 'people' standing next to my bed: one was an unknown woman with one hand on her hip and her head thrown back, and another of a tall, pale and thin, scaly alien-looking figure. The images slowly fade as I examine them, revealing the normal room features behind. I am aware of being awake enough to feel sure the images are real. However, common-sense prevails to reason that I must just dream I am waking and opening my eyes to see the images and that is why, within the dream, I register it as a real event.

THE TORTURE CHAMBER

The following was written before I finally had my own place again in 2014, mercifully reducing this toilet ritual to a manageable level.

I get about three days respite before I have to endure this room again to evacuate my bowels – that is my natural cycle. Because I share the toilet, I ritually clean the seat and the ceramic rim of the bowl with a wad of toilet paper in wipes of factors of four - that is my number. After having defaecated, I go through the unpleasant task of wiping in such a manner that I do not soil my hands or the seat and ensure that I am scrupulously clean. I finally convince myself I am clean enough to re-trouser myself.

I then start the exhaustive checking process: First I check the floor behind and beside the pedestal bowl. I scan small areas of the floor to try and satisfy myself that I have not dropped any paper - soiled or otherwise. The scan is done in sets of fours, and has to be done over and over again every time my concentration is broken by a bad thought or image. These images lie in wait for this moment to pop up and confound me, however hard I try to disallow this. Just lately I am allowing myself to *face the demon,* by doing what I know is the right thing to do - to carry on with the task whilst *actively thinking of the image or the bad thought.* Amazingly it disappears with its tail between its legs, defeated by willpower. Oh how proud I feel in those treasured moments – but it's a scary thing to do.

It is necessary for me to reduce my anxiety enough to go for this trick to *defy the demon,* but once done, I wonder why I hadn't been brave enough to employ this simple obvious trick before. I can now concentrate on checking these pedestal areas are clear, without this hindrance, and feel assured I have done it correctly - *I have defied doubt.* If the thought or image reappears, then I am still sufficiently calm to just let it come. It quickly scurries off or vanishes. Good riddance!

The next procedure involves getting on to my knees to wipe the (already clean) toilet seat. Again, with a wad of four carefully folded sheets, I wipe the seat in a pattern of small scanned areas. Starting at the back, including the hinge, I vigorously wipe the predetermined areas and edges. One, two, three, four - repeating as necessary until I have overlapped all the twelve areas. Although twelve is a 'good' even number divisible by four, there is no other reason for this - it just works out this way in this particular case to naturally complete the process, dependant on the limitations of the toilet seat surface area and my estimated decision of the scan-wipe sub-areas. Then I carefully check the unfolded wad of paper for tell-tale marks - *there never are any* - still not convinced I can leave out this check because it has proved, over and over again, to be a fruitless exercise.

The following stage is very bad for my eyes: I scan the toilet seat areas I have just wiped whilst counting in fours. Every time I cannot stop the intrusive thoughts I have to start again, although I try to employ the *defy the demon doubt* technique whenever I can. At this stage, forcing my mind to concentrate, I find my mind drifting off to envisage pleasurable things I would rather be doing when I finally finish – exhausted. Depending on which light source is available – daylight, electric light or both - I hold my head in a position to allow me to see to check the seat surface with sweeping highlights as additional reassurance that it is indeed clean. Each of these checking tasks can take up to five or ten minutes each. When I am finally able to decide that the checking is complete and *feels right*, I then put the seat up - several times with the *right*, or *no* thought or by *allowing* the thought as a means for it to hopefully vanish.

With the seat up I examine the underside, but strangely without any wiping, unless something was obviously in need of removing. I cannot understand why I allow the underside of the seat to escape the same ritual compulsion, but I don't allow myself to dwell on this - I don't want to invite additional work when I am already weary and achy.

Although my eyes are now tired, I continue my checking: this time the top of the bowl rim, then the inside of the rim; then the sides inside the bowl and finally the sloping sides to the bottom, beneath the water. All on my aching knees. Upon standing up again I quickly lose the numbness and regain the feeling in my legs and feet. I feel the relief that I have nearly finished this unavoidable and utterly exhausting task.

Now for the last stages of the torture chamber experience: the toilet floor complete check. After scanning the toilet mat surround I had been kneeling on, I start the floor scan of *all* of this small room, including the areas around the pedestal I have already checked. It is vinyl flooring in the pattern of six inch square tiles, and it is this pattern I use in this now grid-checking operation.

Starting at the door, I scan and count the four tiles spanning the width of the room. There are actually four and a half tiles, but I am able to absorb this odd half a tile into the first full tile scanning count. Odd I know, but it's a sort of fix to enable an acceptable outcome. The first set of four-tile scans need to seamlessly continue to the next four (and a half) tile set and on to the third and fourth sets. The final set of two four-tile permutations are somewhat different and also have a result-enabling fix. Four room-width tiles run into four remaining part room-length tiles, beside and to the left of the pedestal. This task is accomplished by a four-by-four crossword-type right-angled intersection of the end tiles, counting four and then another four, with one tile at the intersection being counted twice.

How many tiles do I count - not counting the half tiles?

Finally, I consolidate the whole agonisingly ridiculous time-wasting previous hour or so by standing in the open doorway and doing a quick rescan of the two areas of floor, the pedestal mat and the toilet bowl. I then turn away, averting my eyes in a purposeful way as if applying a full-stop to a long sentence. At this point I'm hanging on to the door-frame completely exhausted. I now have about three days before I have to do it all over again! I am compelled to perform all of this despite an increasingly muddled and tired mind.

A mind unable to believe the interpretation of truth provided by my eyes. A strange manifestation of an instant memory loss or self-sabotage.

Perhaps it is just that the serotonin neurotransmitter molecules are unable to traverse the synapse properly or quickly enough.

Perhaps the serotonin receptors become unaccommodating or are blocked, or the serotonin molecules themselves have changed shape to not key-in to the receptors properly.

Perhaps excess time is taken for the flow of electrons to find an alternative neural route to transmit the information, thus bypassing the electrical resistance offered by the ineffectual synaptic gap transition.

Perhaps the time-consuming rerouting through alternative neural networks has to be established to cope with the urgent demand of the electron back-log.

Perhaps it is my inability to collapse the probability wave function (ψ) that maintains an unwanted state of the superposition of two outcomes – suspended uncertainty. I blame it all on Schrödinger!

Perhaps it is none of the above.

23 tiles!

CHAPTER SEVEN

TOO MUCH DETAIL

I exist in a sea of visual and mental detail, continuously assessing, evaluating and analysing everything that assails my senses, *but without the ability to screen-out what is unnecessary or unimportant*. It continues during sleep, except that the images conjured up are even more against my will, manifesting themselves as bad dreams and nightmares. The compulsive rituals within these dreams seem never-ending as I cannot ever resolve them and build up to maddening levels until I finally and thankfully, wake up. Even awake, it is hard to eliminate the still remembered agonising frustration of the the desperate toil endured in the dream - just as often - in the nightmare.

Fear drives my OCD just as it does for those with religious belief with its *scrupulosity*. The fear overwhelms me to the point where I have to deeply immerse myself in compulsive behaviour in a desperate attempt to eliminate it. How much simpler it would be to just ignore it, as I *know* the fear would decline.

Of course, learning to ignore the compulsions is the difficult part of exposure therapy and to be able to control the anxiety to such a low level as to enable self-control and to develop determined willpower to take over and encourage reason.

Being constantly aware of detail around me include noise, light, touch, smell and what I am doing with my arms, legs, head and my mind. When anxious I become linked to objects by what I have termed *eye-strings* to best describe this odd phenomenon. During all of my research over many years I have not heard of anything even remotely similar.

During certain anxious times I am unable to remove my line of sight - the *string* - from a particular object without the inexplicable imagined fear of the taught string dragging on my eyes and the *attached* object. My eyes feel joined to the object by this imaginary string or elastic. Turning my head away only tightens the string and hurts my eyes. I am convinced that if I pull away from the tethered object the action will move or pull it over and that my eyes will be painfully pulled. Indeed, if I deliberately drag my eyes away, tightening the string, I do suffer similar pain in my eye muscles to that expected from a real attached string pulling.

If I am not looking at an object, I cannot know it remains in the same state of being as when I was observing it. However unreasonable this may sound, it is, nevertheless, true. It is similar to the quantum effect of the observed certainty of position reverting to its uncertain, unobserved probability wave.

If, for example, I am checking that a light is off, that is, it is not shining, I can only *truly* know this state of affairs to be the case if I am observing it. *I cannot trust my memory that the light was off the last time I looked*. The result of continual, repeated checking only results in my increased doubt as to its *true state*. After a while I can easily see the dark room *is* lit, as I know from my very recent memory what *that* looks like and so *that* image is created. A red TV/video standby light can truly appear red and glowing even though it is off for the same reason. Even more so in fact, because it is dimmer than a room light when it is illuminated and as a consequence much easier to imagine being on, or in that infuriating state of being on and off at the same time - a sort of Schrödinger superposition effect!

The doubt is naturally brought about by the nature of the ritual repetition of eye movement: *I induce the belief that I cannot know whether it is on or off.*

I try to disengage my eye-string from an object by resorting to trickery, by catching the string off-guard, so to speak, at the fleeting imaginary moment when it is *not* attached to the object. It becomes necessary for me to resort to this trickery in an attempt to try an alternative way out of this binding situation. To actually move away from the object by ripping my eyes off of it, is such a disturbing prospect that I cannot bring myself to attempt it - a bit like committing to the moment one decides to jump from a boat to the shore - that dread fear that you have misjudged the width of the wider-than-you-thought gap.

Even when I succeed with this trick of suddenly looking away from the object when I have a perceived gap in my concentration, I then consider that it was too easy and is therefore probably untrue that I am successfully detached. So, because doubt exists, I return to the relative comfort of re-establishing my full-on, frontal-faced stare at the object, thus reattaching the string - having achieved nothing except more doubt.

Update 2016:

The intensity of the eye-strings compulsion has increased over the years to be a major problem. I need to find a solution to conquer this compulsion which will always require reducing anxiety to a workable level to allow willpower a chance to take control.

The goal is to actively encourage and maintain the power of the will to ignore a compulsion or a repeated compulsion.

Whilst in my obsessive-compulsive anxiety state I can *never know to trust myself* when I have done something correctly, to then allow the task to be abandoned and marked-off as done. The demon doubt is an incredibly powerful force, disabling the sufferer's ability to lead a happy contented life. It is frightening not be in control and letting the aberrations of the mind take over.

OCDers are too close to reality awareness – too intimate, to such an extent that it is revealed as spiky and not the smooth continuous world experienced by the neurotypical – digital rather than analogue, and similar to the uncertain quantum realm of underlying reality particles compared to the comfortable, intuitive and substantial classical reality realm of near certainty.

CHAPTER EIGHT

UNTIL IT FEELS RIGHT

The following was written as a letter in 2002/3 to my daughter in an attempt to explain in detail what I was going through at the time I was living in my Norfolk bungalow. It is reproduced here with some alterations.

Imagine performing any simple everyday task in slow motion: being conscious of every single movement and thought. Imagine holding a thought, which if lost or changed in even the slightest way you would have to start the task all over again. For example: the simple act of flushing the toilet can involve around half-an-hour of aching limbs and tired tortured thoughts. Eyes blink to re-focus or to restart a sequence of 'tries' - the eye-blink acts to reset the situation or part of it. It can be thought of as a shutter on a camera recording an image, the resultant image then fixed as a thought on which to restart the action. In this case to be able to push down the lever to flush the toilet.

I will try to explain it in detail: The very act of reaching my hand out to the lever; the anticipation of the first contact sensation of the texture and temperature of the handle; the attitude of approach and closing proximity to the actual contact; the curling and position of my fingers as the anticipation of the final grasp and push increases my anxiety ten-fold. All of this done whilst not accepting a *wrong image* into my head or a *wrong thought* which will result in my loss of concentration. These thoughts will be of something unpleasant or a key word that instantly puts an undesirable thought or image into my head - just as I attempt to go for the actual push of the handle. Adrenaline is flushing through my body from head to toe like soft electric shocks; sweat pours from my head, my armpits and chest; my hair is wet with sweat trickling down behind my ears.

When I have reached this state it is even harder for me to continue the *tries* at the tortuous attempt to simply flush the toilet. I am acutely aware of other details such as the position of my feet whilst all this is going on; the pressure my feet are exerting on the floor and whether I will scuff the surface should I inadvertently move them. It is an exhausting balancing act of thoughts, feelings and actions.

After the first ten minutes or so, my worn out mind starts to wander to pleasant thoughts, but all the while I am trapped in this statue pose of waiting for the *feeling to be exactly right* to finally go for the lever push. I may risk a 'try' at this time, but at the very millisecond I tense my muscles for the handle-push, my mind tells me it's *not right* and I freeze, unable to continue, plus an extra strong blast of adrenaline running up my neck and head and into my scalp like an electric shock.

This fear is as bad as any other and becomes directed by adrenaline and less by thought. If I go for a push of the handle, it may only go half-way down if I have to abort the action, or it may flush. The devastating fear and disappointment of this occurring when it *wasn't the right moment* and I *wasn't ready*, rapidly increases my anxiety.

An analogy can be made to the risk of running past a gap where you will be shot at immediately you are seen. You can imagine that before you jumped you would hesitate and mentally go through the act of launching yourself across the gap until it *felt right*, because hesitation once you had begun to move would mean you would almost certainly get a bullet. My body and mind state during severe compulsive rituals is often similar to the fear imagined in this example, fuelled by the overwhelming distress of confusion, anxiety and uncertainty.

The rushes of adrenaline that prepare the body and mind instantly into fight or flight mode render the body motionless for a second or two like the proverbial rabbit caught in car headlights. I appreciate that unless you have the anxiety disorder that is OCD, it is impossible to understand why I cannot just *do* the act. If it were *that* simple, OCD wouldn't afflict the millions it does. It is as if *common sense goes out the window.* At times when I am feeling comparatively clear-headed I cannot understand these attacks either! They are elusive, mysterious anomalies of an anxious mind.

Returning to the toilet flushing example (and it is just *one* example of an indefinite number of possible scenarios), imagine I have been successful and have finally managed to push the lever to flush the toilet whilst having an acceptable thought. (It is very difficult, if not impossible when anxious, to have a *blank mind* and go into autopilot so to speak.) Then the doubt sets in: Did I push the lever too hard and strain or damage the internal mechanism? Did I kick out my foot and touch, hit or damage anything whilst concentrating on the lever pull? or Can I keep the good thought intact during the lever's return to its rest position? Does it matter?

By this time I am so physically and mentally exhausted that I am super-sensitised to being obsessive-compulsive until I can get to bed or to somehow rest. I have most likely finally succeeded in completing the task because my mind was insisting that I would feel better than if I went through another attempt - a sort of self-preservation input. Fear gives way to elation as I am finally satisfied that all that torment is over. Then the realisation occurs: What and how do I cope with what I do next?

Continuing the example: I would then have to turn and move my body away from the toilet pedestal and to the door to leave the bathroom. Problems pop into my mind because I am so sensitised to them. If the light pull-switch was on, I am compelled to go through a similar sequence of thoughts and actions as I did for the toilet lever to enable me to switch it off.

I inevitably catch a glimpse of myself in the bathroom mirror which causes an instant reaction I was not expecting, resulting in yet another adrenaline flush. These become almost painful in a manner similar to enduring hiccups for hours. Then I bob my head and its reflection in and out of the mirror until I have the *right movement and moment* when my expression *didn't look sinister,* whilst at the same time balancing a *good* or *right* thought. I can usually execute this ritual quite quickly because averting my eyes from the mirror is usually quite easy for me.

This was a time when eye-strings weren't such a problem as they have been in the last few years.

Then there is the task of trying to open the bathroom door. I usually leave the door ajar to make it easier for me, but nevertheless, when I am in this state I am compelled to go through the reaching out, grasping and pulling the handle compulsion yet again. On opening, the edge of the door reveals a new line of sight that is interpreted as an interruption in my much-needed flow of action. Hesitation produces a freeze situation, whereupon I will then have to re-evaluate all I have just gone through in the bathroom.

This may result in my return to the flush lever obsession, only to start the compulsive ritual procedure all over again in the remembered order, including the thoughts at the time during the original lever push; then my moving from the pedestal and the mirror, the light pull-switch and opening the door. The longer it takes to execute, the harder it becomes - as always.

Back at the door, having to part open and close it again as it was the last time, will involve leaving the door at a certain *comfortable* angle, to satisfy myself that I have not banged the door on the wall-mounted heater. Then, when the door ritual is done, still it continues.

Now there is the anticipation of moving into the new space of the hall by overcoming the threshold. Which body attitude do I adopt to initialise the move out of the bathroom and into the hallway? Which foot I use first is established quite quickly. Imagine yourself starting a stair-climb on the *wrong-feeling foot,* indeed try it - it will feel awkward. Many analogies can be applied here, such as *getting out of bed on the wrong side* - hence the sarcastic comment: 'Got out of the wrong side of the bed this morning?' to someone who appears to be grumpy and finding it difficult to cope in the morning.

Passing over thresholds is difficult for me because they represent a pronounced change - one room setting *with all its detail* for another. Movement doesn't flow automatically for me as it does when I'm feeling relatively good, or as it is for normal people. I plan where my feet will end up on the floor when I move. I am held as if by an invisible tether - unable to move until I can decide to initiate a movement, and this can happen in countless other situations. The eventual transition from the bathroom space to the hall space only presents me with the next threshold into the next room space. I carefully consider what my feet or arms may knock if they should flail - they don't, *but I know they could*, and because of that I plan my movements ahead of actually doing them, along with tentative practice attempts, like choreography for some play or musical with the staccato-like repeat action similar to a verbal stutter.

Although I am now finally out of the bathroom, I am moving in a deliberate robotic fashion whilst slipping into thoughts of all the pleasurable pursuits I long to get on with instead of an anxious compulsive ritual session. It becomes that I *so* want to be doing something else that the OC becomes sadistically more intense. This state of mind is so *ridiculously unreasonable and against all common sense*, but remains an uncontrollable result of a full-blown OC session.

When I'm having a relatively good anxiety-free time, I cannot understand why I allow myself to continually fall so easily into the clutches of OCD. It is like a one-way system, so easy to enter but next to impossible to leave; a black hole of the mind which might radiate away with time.

The need to eat, drink, to sit down or even to think clearly gradually replaces the overwhelming needs of the OC behaviour. I may, by now, be adopting some sort of automatic flow with my actions and not thinking and analysing everything as much. I may have missed a TV documentary I really wanted to see, but precisely because I was conscious I may miss it if the rituals in the bathroom continued, this added anxiety just exacerbates and compounds the problem, an extra component pressure to compromise my so-needed concentration required to complete the task.

I plan well ahead to use the toilet before a TV program I would like to see, and it is so disappointing if I need to go just before or during a program, because I know I will have great difficulty in returning, if at all. Also, I can still hear the TV and feel even more crestfallen as the images formed in my mind from the sound are a frustrating poor substitute for the real thing. On some occasions I will force myself back into the sitting room to see the continuing program rather than to miss it. This has a big downside: Not only will I not be able to concentrate on the rest of the program because of the unfinished ritual being on my mind as *saved* for later on, but I also know it will be harder to complete when the time comes. Also, other compulsive rituals will plague me more than they would have if I wasn't putting another on hold, and will build up into a mental back-log of many rituals waiting to be processed.

By the late evening I am very tired, with my ability to confront my compulsions greatly reduced. I have difficulty getting out of my chair for fear that my sudden push to arise will mean I may damage something that may even be on the far side of the room, such as the TV or hi-fi. The remote controls are on the sofa or the coffee table beside me and present a big problem when I need to get up. If I knock the coffee table for instance, there is a whole ritual involved in repositioning it on the carpet, *even if on close inspection I can see it has not moved.* The ritual involves having the *right thought* as I lift the table up whilst I am sitting down and *continuing to hold that thought* as I carefully attempt to replace the legs without dragging them over the tufts of the carpet pile. Even if I feel I have done it right, doubt instantly takes a hold and I will repeat it again and again, each time with increased difficulty. I sit to move the table because I feel that if I were standing it would be so easy to swing the table into the TV, even though it would take several steps to reach it. So, if I sit, it negates that additional problem.

These compulsions to complete the rituals cause great physical discomfort to me because of the statue-like positions I hold during these periods – sometimes for a total of two hours a day. I suffer shoulder, back and neck ache that only add to the misery. After a bad day my bed is an escape as it was for four solid years from 1996 to 2000.

As I'm sure my reader can imagine from all of the above, I cannot just go to bed, because even minimal preparations can be rife with ritual. The simple act of switching off the TV by the remote standby button requires me to sit at the edge of the sofa and to bring my thoughts and actions together to be able to touch the button without the adrenaline-fuelled doubt that I will scrabble up the rubber buttons with my fingernails. The position I adopt with my hand to push this standby button means that the heel of my hand is in contact with the surface of the cloth-covered sofa. Because of this I am conscious of my hand leaving the surface with the attendant doubts as to whether I have scuffed the surface nap direction; this results in repeated smoothing-over and tapping-counting actions *until I feel it is right.* But why do I think it matters? That is the enigma!

Incidentally, there is no way to create a standard definition for when an action or thought 'feels right'.

This *right feeling* is dependant on so many factors which can be interlinked and interdependent and which are entirely specific to the situation and to the individual. I think of it as more like the ability to create an emotion on demand. It would be difficult to create a feeling of anger, sadness, joy, guilt or jealousy on demand, although I believe actors are taught this skill. I know all of this behaviour is nonsense and that none of it actually matters; us OCDers are not mad or stupid – we just *think too much and cannot filter out trivia*. This is the anxious, overwhelming, dark doubt that is OCD.

To continue: I need to be sitting down to do this TV-off compulsion because this limits my movement, reducing the likelihood of the fear I may knock or suddenly flail into something. After I have successfully switched off the TV, I may feel I am going to abort an attempt at getting up and will suddenly sit back down again because I cannot hover – it is too much of an uncertain position. Objects which I cannot remove from the immediate area (as this involves getting up) such as my spectacles, mobile phone, TV remote control and such like, I feel are at great risk of being sat on, damaged or broken. This is an irrational fear too, as the times I have sat on things (very rarely) have not caused me any great worry at all; it is the *fear* of the damage that is the problem. Once up from the chair I follow the pre-planned first few steps that I have also been concentrating on before I got up. This is important to the ritual because this is the act that will ensure I am well away from the sofa and any possible damage that might result if I hesitate.

Hesitation is an inbuilt OCD fear for me because it will inevitably mean a compulsion will be instantly initiated in this action-thought gap - *precisely* when I don't want it.

Sometimes, when I am feeling all right and quite cheerful I can miraculously get up with hardly a thought, *simply because I am in a relaxed state of mind, more confident and less likely to hesitate.*

The preparation for bed continues, as once out of the chair there are the thresholds to confront once again. At this point in the sequence of pre-bed events I can usually cope with passing over thresholds, with only a fleeting thought not to worry and that it is easier to ignore them if I can. I check the back door is locked about four times minimum and press against the locked handle with so much force that I fear I will break it and not be able to lock it – the irony! Leaving it broken and unlocked is not so much the worrying problem, but the fact I will have to get someone up to fix it if I was unable to do so. Apart from the cost, the problem is that I will have to speak on the phone, and later have to speak with someone in my house, each event which I would have to relive over and over again to satisfy myself that I had not said anything wrong, stupid or ambiguous which might upset them or me. Of course, being so anxious and preoccupied with the fear of appearing odd is precisely the conditions to achieve it.

This door handle pushing down ritual to repeatedly feel it is locked remains a big problem for me and has resulted in three internal mechanism handle breaks in two years. I can only truly know it is locked if I can maintain the hard feel of it being locked. When I let go I am uncertain because of lack of evidence, and remembering it was locked last time I pushed plays no part as it was instantly erased from my memory – a sort of self-inflicted sabotage.

Then it's to the fridge for my drink, deliberately mindful when pouring it from the carton that I do not spill any, as that would involve a dishcloth wiping ritual. I replace the carton in the fridge door shelf in just the *right position* – label at the front with the carton's front side parallel to the shelf edge and equidistant from the other objects on the shelf, checking the lid is snapped shut by pushing down on it, simultaneously assessing the degree of creak made by the plastic shelf it sits on to ensure it wasn't at breaking point. I then close the fridge door, hopefully without the line of sight eclipse problem mentioned earlier. To avoid this I always perform a slow deliberate blink and turn my head slightly away to the side just at the split-second I would have seen the eclipse of the object inside by the door edge. If the door is pushed shut too hard or too softly then I am compelled to repeat the closure several times until it *feels and sounds just right*. If I close it too hard I will open it again to check the drink carton has not come open or leaked. If I close it too softly I will do it again, and if the door doesn't close completely I have to open it wider and then push it shut again with the *correct* click of the magnetic door strip against the frame until it *feels right*.

If I do this task when I'm not anxious I hardly think about it and I get it right first time or am happy to leave it. Carrying the drink to the bedroom can be tricky, as I must concentrate on not feeling I am going to spill or throw the contents whilst at the same time walking through doorways and over thresholds. Surprisingly, I manage this most times without concern; I think it is because, by now, I am so intent on getting to bed to rest.

I do not close any internal doors for ease of movement and to avoid door compulsions. I then undress in the dim bedroom without switching the light on because I leave the curtains partly open to let in the daylight and would also have trouble switching it off again. To open and close them each day would unnecessarily tempt a compulsive ritual because I fiddle with them to get them hanging *just right.* I also feel uneasy that people could see me doing this and that they would think I was spying on them.

My clothes are folded *just right* and placed on the chair. I vaguely remember how good it felt to just throw them on the chair at the time when I thought I had finally overcome the OCD during CBT. Then it's over the bedroom-hallway threshold again to try to put the hall light switch off and to finally get into bed to settle down to sleep with usually quite a clear mind. Switching off the hall light can take quite a considerable effort, involving balancing my thoughts and the switch lever movement, and then there is the final threshold to cross back into the bedroom and into bed. Peace at last you might think - no such luck! It is then a different trial that my exhausted mind has to face - *the dreams and nightmares.*

My dreams are deeply troublesome each and every night, as I am dealing with the worst *virtual obsessions and compulsions*. It is as if my whole OC memory bank lets loose all of its contents to dominate and control all of my dreams. As each of around four dreams per my time in bed develops, I become increasingly unconsciously anxious and wake up in a sweat with most of the images intact. Then I am compelled to concentrate hard to recall and relive all the individual OC events that peppered each dream.

The dreams are always complex and often involve my children when they were young and my former wife. I assess each event that troubles me over and over again until it *feels right.* I may relive most of a dream, but then become stuck on one seemingly unresolvable compulsive-ritualistic event within it. The more I concentrate to resolve it, the more likely it is that I will have to start at the beginning of the dream all over again; this can happen several times for each dream.

The most devastating and demanding task occurs after gathering a back-log of dreams waiting to be analysed, because even if one dream is resolved I will go back over it again if I get stuck on another. I feel as if I am going mad with images flashing in my mind from all the dreams, because I've *learnt* them by reliving them in every detail I can remember so many times. I remain mentally exhausted even when I'm asleep and feel unable to get up until I have completed all the analysis to my satisfaction.

Because I am so tired I find it almost impossible to clear all the dreams before the next day arrives and finally force myself out of bed when I feel I have had enough glimpses of the fact that the dreams were not real. I have little control over this part-unconscious dream analysis, but again, I am compelled to check that I haven't said or done anything to worry about and that I am not a bad person. I consider: Where was I? What was I doing? Who was I with? What did I say? What did they think? What was their reaction? Did I make a fool of myself or say something out of place? If I have had to go to the (real) toilet during a dream or a dream analysis, I become so uncertain of what I'm doing or where I am that I again get stuck in rituals, especially thresholds.

Exhausted, I get up late in the day and make it to the kitchen for coffee and just sit at the table trying to come out of the dream state. I read something until I realise that I am truly awake and that nothing in the dreams were real. During this time, if the doorbell or the telephone ringing interrupts me, I am again plunged into doubt and have to go over the conversations I may have had at the door or on the telephone, plus the niggling doubt about the dreams again resurfacing. These agonising mental gymnastics can take up most of what is left of my day.

The feeling of elation I get when I finally feel free of all this worry is wonderful - but short lived. I yearn to feel unburdened and unencumbered by all this waste of time taking up most of my life. I am always tired and feel worn out, and because of that I am susceptible to worry about anything that doesn't run to plan during the day.

It is very difficult for me to be able to go out without great problems, but if I have previously had a reasonably good day and night I do manage to do some shopping. If I have a fixed appointment (doctor or dentist etc.) and it falls on a day in the middle of a bad time, I have to cancel. Many times during trips into town I come over feeling terribly weak and faint and start to hover around in shop doorways looking suspicious, trying to remember where I'm supposed to be going next or to continually check my wallet to ensure my money and bank card are safe.

When I return to my car I sit for a while to gather my wits and put all the accumulated niggling thoughts and doubts on hold if I cannot resolve them quickly. Luckily I don't have any driving OCs to contend with and the only car-related problems are getting in and out - with that push out of the seat problem again; turning the lights off, on and off again if they've been on; winding the driver's door window up and down and up until it *feel right* if it's been open and checking the handbrake is on the *right click* and not on too hard. Also, getting my *mind right* to press the remote locking button on my key is a problem because I feel I may scratch the paintwork with the attached keys at the very moment I press the button, despite the obvious fact that because it is remote locking I can do it away from the car, except that I have to see the driver's door ledge button go down as the lock clicks and the direction indicator signals flash. I will still continue to stare with strained tired eyes at the now recessed door lock button to reinforce my belief that the doors are indeed locked. Actually trying all the handles is a miserable way to go, because each handle has its own feel and sound to get *exactly right*. Pulling the hatchback door down is troublesome because outside my house I freeze up because I think people are watching me. As I have said, common sense goes right out the window with OCD - indeed if common sense prevailed I wouldn't *have* OCD.

Disabling doubt that things are *not done right* seems to be the force that controls those with OCD.

[Explaining to Aimie in this letter: Research has shown this doubt may happen because of a lack of the neurotransmitter serotonin being available that is necessary to pass information from one neuron to the next via the synapse. Medicating with Selective Serotonin Re-uptake Inhibitors (SSRIs) help prevent the serotonin molecules from being reabsorbed, and therefore renders them more readily available across the synapses to pass on the information. Perhaps, when the electrical message pathway has bad connections like this, the message information becomes corrupted. Since this happens through millions of brain cells every second, it is amazing that even the normal process works as well as it does.

A good analogy here is the computer doing strange things (compulsive rituals) or crashing (nervous breakdown) when it is overloaded with tasks, but we don't consider the machine a freak because of it, even though it may be thrown out the window along with common sense!]

I have experienced the anxiety-induced inability to speak properly on the telephone (2002) when I am so anxious that when I attempt to force out the words I lose my voice for a short, but embarrassing time, as stress causes my vocal chords to seize up and shorten producing a higher pitch.

I may get a couple of days respite from these full-on obsessive-compulsive episodes when I am actually able to nearly enjoy myself and to be able to indulge in my hobbies - *but the suffocating doubt and exhaustion always return*. I am even punished when I occasionally have a good day. If I wake up having coped with the time in bed, then I can move forward with confidence and plan ahead with excitement at the feeling of freedom being released from the chains of OCD in my prison home. I plan to go out, to play guitar or make those telephone calls I was putting off for fear of saying the wrong thing or drying up mid-conversation. A bad telephone conversation often causes me days of added torment, as I continually try to re-evaluate the evidence that it went fine and was acceptably normal or not.

Pleasurable pursuits always take second priority to OCD.

It is as if I have to give myself permission of the highest order before I am worthy of participating in anything remotely enjoyable.

All the enjoyable things I want to do flood into my mind on my 'day off' and I become so excited that I do things in a hyper speeded-up sort of way: I eat, read, and think at 100 mph, with the feeling that I want to accomplish things almost before I have started them. Eating becomes a race, and as a result I cannot enjoy my food. I read so fast that I stumble over the words, although quite often there is an unexpected benefit in that I can speed-read, or that I *think* I can! This feels great, as I am able to move forwards along the text quickly without the gruelling hesitation characterised by obsessive doubt and the compulsive rituals are pushed aside for once. At these times I feel my mind is freed and that I have the power to keep it that way. I re-evaluate the OC behaviour wondering why I give in to it so easily.

I think of being among the trees and hearing birdsong on a bright *crisp* day (I become terribly anxious and cannot cope when I am hot because the heat doubles my stress). I imagine going for a drive to the coast or going to town to look in the shops without a care in the world. I am swamped with good feelings of how things could and should be for me.

Oftentimes, I am faced with such a choice of things I can do because I feel so much better, that I almost freeze and don't get on with any of them. The result of having a couple of consecutive good days is that I subsequently suffer a couple of bad days. The feeling of freedom on those good days is countered by the equally bad following days; but bad periods can last weeks with no respite whatsoever and I lose the will to live.

It may seem that I am exaggerating or over-detailing my plight, *but this is not so*. In fact, if I detailed *all* my obsessive thoughts and resulting compulsions that I experience each day, it would at least double my descriptions presented here; so what you read isn't the half of it.

I'd like my *normal* reader [and my daughter reading this in the original letter] to imagine all the things they do during a typical working day, the week and the year. From the mundane unconscious acts of walking, talking, eating, washing, dressing and going to the toilet, to being able to go out to work and earn money (something I wish that I can do again someday) and to be interacting with people relatively effortlessly. Spending leisure time with others and being able to laugh properly. All the actions and interactions of a normal person's day, in the most part, are taken for granted. There may be things that were done or said that bothered them for a while, but are then quickly and naturally resolved, forgotten and dismissed as just being human and entirely normal.

[This is the end of the modified letter to Aimie.]

I wanted to share my experiences here in print in the hope that non-sufferers (neurotypicals) can glimpse what it is like to live with anxiety and Obsessive Compulsive Disorder. I am certain I have Asperger's Syndrome and seem to exist on another plane, *an intricate dimension of underlying reality that is all pervading*. I think continually in an over-deep manner, analysing - forever analysing.

I see only detail instead of the big picture, analogous for a neurotypical person viewing the smooth ocean from a great height when I see the reality of the crashing waves and chaos up close and are disturbed by their innate uncertainty; also analogous to a wheel rolling over the bumps and cracks when I am a small wheel and troubled by them. I look at and think of everything from different angles and points of view. I am over-sensitive, in fact super-sensitive, to light, sound, smell, taste, touch, thoughts and actions and everything else around and within me.

Because of this heightened sensitivity I feel acutely aware of realities and existences I cannot see or experience: the gargantuan immensity of the universe and the infinitesimal sub-atomic elementary particles of the quantum world - and everything in between. These macroscopic and microscopic realms, those bigger and those smaller than ourselves, merge seamlessly as one universal size gradient through us – the observer. The quantum realm requires different (probability) rules to enable us to describe it compared to the classical Newtonian realm, but the fact that we detect an enigmatic discontinuity must be significant. This point is the quantum-classical transition. Could it be the point where gravity ceases to be an influence on the tiny? I digress!

CHAPTER NINE

COMMON SENSE OUT THE WINDOW

You know how it is when you get a song or a phrase *on the brain,* it can be maddening – like hiccups; it can go on and on for hours by which time you feel ill. Thoughts, words, music or images can constantly go around in my head like several TV channels all on at once, an audio-visual psychedelic cacophony where it is almost impossible to think straight. It is a bit like a waking dream because I cannot stop it. As I have mentioned, when a computer is overloaded with tasks it runs slower and finally freezes-up – analogous to a human nervous breakdown. ***OCD is like a continuous nervous breakdown*** where gross anxiety, doubt and confusion take control over common sense. OCD doesn't recognise or respect common sense and leaves me to cope as best I can. Repetition and hesitation are the main disablers, repeating tasks until either I am sure they are done properly or I have had to give up and try to organise getting to bed, tired and confused with exhaustion, the doubted task being put aside for replay analysis when I am next clear-minded enough.

OC corrupted tasks can be anything: The need to adjust a piece of paper to be just how I *feel* it must lie; re-reading the line in a book, flicking my eyes back and forth, side to side, to try to cancel a bad thought or image and to then try again, all in quick succession, thus developing a nervous twitch. Turning the page of a book is fraught with difficulty as it is like switching a switch; the next page is another block of text with different words that may trigger a bad thought. In fact they always do, but I am not able to ignore it and so it interrupts my reading flow. The page is then turned back and forth until it *feels comfortable* to continue. To continue reading without employing this cancelling device makes it almost impossible to take in the meaning or order of the following words and sentences.

This problem is with me now as I try to type this text. This is such an uncomfortable feeling that it is easier and quicker to go back and retry the cancelling compulsion until it *feels right* to continue, whereupon my mind is freed for a few more sentences, and so my progress across the printed or typed page is jerky and uncertain, missing subtle meanings. I will sometimes remember a problem word that occurred a few pages back and again get that awful feeling that *something is not right* to allow me to continue. Reading words freely and smoothly only happens rarely when I am feeling very calm. Another compulsion is to repeatedly check the next page is numerically sequential to the previous page.

It is not only reading the words of a sentence that is a struggle to keep continually flowing. Ordinary tasks such as making a cup of instant coffee present a similar problem. This task, like any other, is a series of steps that normal folk continue through without the *bump* of each next step. Each step is done one by one with equal attention until the *right feeling* is experienced. The level of difficulty depends on my mood and how tired I am feeling at the time. The task can take place very rapidly, maintaining momentum without the *dreaded hesitation* catalysing a doubt. I must ensure the kettle is seated on the stand exactly and then I move the kettle with the stand a short distance back and forth four times along the worktop to allow me to sense there is equal tension either side of the feet in contact with the work-surface, ensuring balance and symmetry. I feel acutely aware of the particles and molecules at the interface of the stand's feet and the plastic worktop adjusting to the frictional force by the movement I cause; all this done whilst in fear of a thought compelling me to repeat the action.

Preparing the coffee and sugar in the cup, each has to be done without a bad thought or image and without spilling anything or knocking the cup or jars. If I knock or touch something unplanned I will purposely add my number of knocks to total four or eight, as previously stated. If *that* goes wrong I will start the knocks from the beginning, hopefully only four because this is brief, balanced and started anew. If during these four knocks I *feel uncomfortable,* then I can momentarily ignore this and continue quickly, almost in a token manner to complete four sets of four knocks.

Why 4, you might ask?

Well, 1 is odd and only once; 2 is balanced as it is even but not enough; 3 is again not an even number – so, no odd numbers at all!

4 is enough, and even, and so ideal.

No number 5.

Half of 6 is 3, so it has an odd and therefore uncertain number associated with it.

No number 7.

8 is the second OK number.

The four sets of 4 are balanced and still maintain the number 4, but 16 is too big a number and so back to try just 4 again if I am uncomfortable with 16!

Makes perfect sense doesn't it!

All this effort for pointless detail. But that is precisely what my OCD is: a compulsion for ensuring detail is correct every step of the way, if not, I don't feel in control, *which I think is the heart of OCD.* I dwell on detail and miss the big picture. *I do not trust myself* to feel I have done things properly and feel that if I don't ensure this then I will be persecuted by thoughts of being imperfect and therefore not worthy of anything.

Always being in doubt as to whether I have done something properly to my satisfaction, I repeat the act until it *feels right* even though I cannot explain what '*feels right*' actually means. A sort of brief respite analogous to the space at the end of a sentence or paragraph.

This 'until it feels right' is the one thing I need to ignore to be on the road out of my OC hell. It's obviously got to 'feel wrong' and to carry on regardless! Easy to say.

All I feel certain of is that it feels terribly awkward, a fear that everything else I subsequently do will be wrong unless I get this thing right in my mind. It is more than that: it is *fear, panic and dread* that drive this process, producing almost painful rushes of adrenaline through my body and prickling my scalp. How do I know when something is done properly, or well enough to leave it? I know it must lie somewhere between anxious perfectionism and slovenly complacency! Until it feels right? It never feels right! How do I know? I cannot draw on common sense because it somehow becomes inaccessible to me just when I need it!

It's like a glitchy robot repeating an action because it has faulty feedback that the action was undertaken successfully. It cannot decide whether it was done correctly or needs to be repeated? So, why can't I rely on my experience of performing that particular type of action? I should have learnt it by now! Why do I doubt my ability? Why must I compulsively distrust myself?

It is as if one side of my brain actively sabotages the other. There is a condition known as AgCC where the developing brain's corpus callosum is not formed or only partially formed (agenesis) in the foetus. The corpus callosum is the primary connection linking the two cerebral hemispheres by a broad band of nerve fibres. Individuals who have had the corpus callosum cut to divide the two hemispheres can display *Anarchic Hand* or *Alien Hand Syndrome*, whereby the non-dominant hand (usually the left hand) will unconsciously undo what the other has done – such as unbuttoning the dominant hand's buttoning of their shirt.

It is perfectly normal and natural to repeat an action you feel wasn't quite right. You might understandably recheck the baby seat buckle is secure – *even though you know you did it correctly the first time,* because it is not something you are prepared to leave until you have reinforced the near-certainty that it is secure by repetition. The memory of the action must be burned into your conscious awareness of *now*.

So, why do I need to repeat the tightening of a bottle top when it has no real importance compared to my child's safety seat buckle?

I can only conclude that all my actions must be compulsively rigorous and are not at all dependant on their importance; they must all come up to the same standard of excellence to ensure I minimise all possibility of mistakes.

Low self-esteem is the result of my feelings of uncertainty about my thoughts and actions; it is the same with almost everything I do. I plan how to walk across a room, then if it doesn't go to plan I can be swamped by an adrenaline rush of panic and freeze, often resulting in recreating my steps either physically or mentally. At later times I may feel compelled to replay the scenario in my mind, just like re-running a video sequence, pausing and reviewing until I am sure I didn't miss anything; it is an exhausting process. Sometimes when retracing my steps across a room it *feels horribly wrong* and impossible to move my feet either back or forward, leaving me statuesque and often unable to balance. When I fall I try desperately to keep my feet in the same position (as in the contortional floor game with coloured circles for the hands and feet on a large printed plastic sheet). This position will be maintained for minutes, even hours, despite my pain and numbness until I *feel it is all right* to move; but I never know how I finally get permission to move. It is most likely that after an hour or so tiredness clouds my memory giving me an unexpected window of opportunity to grab at my chance for freedom. I may try this trick to outwit the compulsion several times without success and then have to reassess the position of my feet relative to the furniture, to again go through the process of *removing the doubt* that I have kicked, damaged or even just knocked something - anything. I plan my escape route to the door, and when I finally reach the safety of the next room I can then look forward to the numbness and pain in my feet and legs ebbing away and my mind clearing.

If many of these saved, unresolved compulsive tasks build up in my mind as a back-log, it can sometimes be days before I am satisfied that all I did afterwards was not affected adversely and finally realise that everything *was* all right and that I *need not have worried*. Ironically, I cannot think of a single case where wilfully *not* dwelling on a thought or action resulted in anything untoward, yet I cannot be convinced and I don't know why! *I know* I didn't knock or damage anything in the room or say anything wrong or ambiguous to someone; in fact when I do, I certainly know about it! *Still* I am not convinced that I do not have to worry and that I do not have to give in to the demands to compulsively ritualise to these unreasonable obsessions.

It is as if I develop an instant memory-loss of things I have just done – prompting me to repeat them, but only to forget that feeling of completion once again.

I am throwing out any chance that I can trust I did it right or well enough the first time and that it must, almost automatically, result in a ritual re-enactment. I repeat the memory recall a minimum of four times, and if anything interrupts my train of thought during any of the four replays then I have to start again at one and be sure that each recall was identical. I am not flexible enough to cope with unplanned changes, and so, if for instance the telephone rings or there is a knock at the door when I am mid-ritual, I feel a desperate panic overwhelm me. Do I try to answer the telephone call or the knock at the door in a terrible state, over-riding the compulsion not to move, or do I ignore the caller and worry that it might have been an important life-or-death situation that I may have missed? This sudden new event interrupting my tired and confused mind will add to my back-log of tasks to resolve, or result in distress during my sleep, mingling with my disturbing dreams and nightmares, not allowing me to be able to tell what is real or a dream.

I am well aware I have *learnt* to feel and react as I do and live in the resulting constant fear. With wrong-thinking, I have created neuron pathways of a memory of each scenario experienced which is recalled whether I want it or not.

The tragedy of OCD is that those who suffer these bizarre and disturbing experiences are intelligent people who know full well that none of this obsessive-compulsive repetition and false bad feelings matter, but it is experienced and has its own reality about it.

This absurd, illogical, time-wasting behaviour devastates my life as it does for the millions of other sufferers across the world. It is *learned* behaviour that has to be *unlearned* before any progress to normality can be achieved. Employing cognitive behavioural techniques and exposure therapy encourage repetition of the *right* way to do things, despite the awful dread feeling that it is incorrect and very wrong; it builds *new* neuron pathways to allow the wrong ones to dismantle and dissolve. The problem with this is that *I do not know the right way to do things*, especially as everyone's way of doing things is slightly different to achieve the same result.

It is only the consensus of opinion that is the optimum right way of doing things.

I do not know the normal way to go about dealing with thoughts and actions because I have suffered OCD since a young child. All of my unnatural behaviour makes getting through each day an ordeal, always fearing the next compulsion.

Fear fills my days and fills my dreams and fuels my anxiety and OCD.

When a compulsive ritual is inevitable in the presence of other people, they cannot of course understand, because if they *did* they would have OC tendencies themselves. In fact I fear explaining it in painful detail in case the person is anxious themselves with a predisposition to acquire this knowledge and to negatively respond to it. I believe it is possible to create doubt where once certainty reigned.

Getting through every minute of every day for a lifetime has been torture for me and I do not know how I have survived its devastation. I feel that I won't fear death because it will be a wonderful release from a life of torment and misery.

OCD has destroyed me and disallowed maintaining a close relationship with others. I suffer the demons of doubt - dark doubt - dark dreams - even doubting my own worth to exist.

Pleasurable pursuits are few and far between for these reasons: I have no OC-free time, despite other people *wondering what I do all day;* I feel I shouldn't be enjoying myself as I have so many chores that are more important; I feel I do not deserve to enjoy myself because others have suffered who had to live with me; I seem unable to *let myself go* in order to allow myself to be in the necessary mood in which to be happy or contented.

I so very much look forward to relaxing cosy in my bed after each day's tormenting trials. At the same time I know what the night will bring. I have disturbing dreams that are full of virtual obsessions and compulsive rituals dragged from my memory of bad experiences. They manifest themselves into countless permutations of scenarios that my unconscious mind forces me to endure.

The times I am asleep are often worse than my waking hours, because when awake I have at least *some* control over my mind - not much, but some. I have no way of limiting the psychological damage the dreams do to me; I cannot go to bed and just sleep it off! I frequently talk, shout and sweat my way from one OC *dreamare* to the next, unable to satisfactorily conclude them. They build up during the night and I remain in bed until mid-day or later whilst trying to sort out the dreams as if they were real events. I cannot simply get up and forget them - how I wish I could! *[Update: I can now do this.]*

When I wake I am lying there compelled to go through each dream to try and resolve the remembered obsessive-compulsive situations. I cannot just get out of bed because everything I do subsequently *feels terribly wrong* – often sinister.

Night time visits to the toilet are a great struggle as I am fighting off thoughts and images flying at me from within. Concentrating on getting up, walking, opening doors and every step of the way is fraught with trying to remember everything I am doing in case I have to recall it later. This will include trying not to go through the flush handle and light switch problems detailed in the preceding chapter. I do not know which way to turn, literally, and keep questioning myself: Did I do that right? Does it matter? No, it doesn't but I've got to do it anyway! Then I continue the best I can back to my bed. I can be up for a few minutes or an hour standing around trying to convince my tired troubled mind that it is all right to get back into bed. I am trying to sort out my mind from the dreams and the half-awake movements I went through to reach the toilet and back. This will include concentrating hard on pulling open and closing the bed covers because of the eclipsing effect I have mentioned earlier.

Tiring eye-strings, parallax and blinking are always present.

Finally, back in bed, I return easily into the OC dreams - I have no other sort as far as I know. After more possible trips to the toilet from my bed during the night and the next day, I have a build-up of dream memories to replay to ensure that during them I did everything *all right.* Sometimes I can ignore them and it is such a relief that I am sure for once that I do not have to spend more time going through them. It is at this point that my mind may again wander to pleasurable things I would rather be doing.

To face the next day is my primary challenge, when I finally *feel it is all right* to get up and decide I can cope; but I am so tired because my mind never rests. Pleasurable pursuits are rare and I don't feel comfortable with them because I think I should be compulsively ritualising over some thought I have forgotten about. It is as if I am so attuned to OC behaviour that the rare times I am not involved with it soon give way to reverting to some unwanted thoughts again. I may get away with a couple of hours of relative enjoyment at best.

I regularly go through conversation replays in my mind to convince myself that I have not said anything wrong, rude or ambiguous. One conversation may be repeated over and over again because I fear I may have missed something - because I have before. It is with great effort that I try to drag the different phrases, words and facial expressions from my memory. The same goes for recalling my behaviour whilst with others as a *virtual audio-video replay* in case I did something that was unacceptable but had not realised it at the time. I struggle to twist my mind around to put myself in the other person's position to see how my words and actions would have seemed to them. This process is made worse because I cannot know their mind and so cannot interpret their feelings. Just when I think I'm convinced that it was all right and have nothing to worry about, a shutter falls to prevent me concluding. As a result I feel I have done the best I can and the memory eventually fades.

CHAPTER TEN

COMPUTER PROGRAM ANALOGY FOR EXPOSURE THERAPY AND NEURAL REGROWTH

Imagine unwanted feedback loops developing in the brain's active neural network which become an easier, less resistive pathway to follow, resulting in compulsion – a helter-skelter impulse cascade of involuntary repetition.

It can be thought of as impulsively following a well trodden-down path through a cornfield, one which was not the best or quickest way through, but is easier to follow because it apparently shows the way, but instead leads you back. It is very hard to ignore this pathway, but the desired alternative is to carefully, thoughtfully and purposefully work out the best way across the field of corn to your intended destination and to then tread it over and over again until it gradually becomes the impulsive choice to make; to determinedly emphasise its permanence over the wrong, now discarded pathway, which will overgrow and become benign.

Neural plasticity allows for neural regrowth. For example the following small program in BASIC could be analogous.

```
10  START  task or thought
20  CONTINUE
30  DOUBT  not done correctly
40  GOTO 10  x4or8 (repetition) until FEELS RIGHT
50  FEELS RIGHT so CONTINUE
60  BAD THOUGHT: GOTO 10  repeat until FEELS RIGHT
70  FEELS RIGHT so CONTINUE to END
80  END  task or thought
90  STOP
100 FEELS RIGHT
```

In this analogy, exposure therapy, ET (the intention to create and reaffirm a new, better path through the corn) can correct a faulty program by inserting command line 35, which will ignore &/or delete lines 40 & 60 in this example. An additional ET line 90 stops repetition.

This following programming example in 1980s BASIC uses increments of ten to allow for modification of the program function and result by inserting up to 9 additional lines between any increment of 10.

Exposure therapy described by steps in BASIC programming to encourage neural plasticity would look something like this:

```
10  START  task or thought
20  CONTINUE
30  DOUBT  not done correctly
      35  (ET insert) GOTO 70 (willpower to ignore and finally
       delete lines 40 & 60)
40  GOTO  10
50  FEELS RIGHT so CONTINUE to END
60  BAD THOUGHT: GOTO 10 repeat until FEELS RIGHT
70  FEELS RIGHT so CONTINUE to END
80  END  task or thought
      90  (ET insert) STOP  thoughts of returning to 10
100 FEELS RIGHT
```

Neuroplasticity is the process of change to the neuron structures and functioning of the brain through repeated positive experiences (ET) and the conscious use of directed thoughts – rewiring. But in my experience this is only possible when stress and the resultant anxiety is reduced to a manageable level; but, with no support or encouragement at home this was a serious challenge which I only just succeeded in partly overcoming.

CHAPTER ELEVEN

CHECKING, EYE-STRINGS AND OTHER STUFF

When I am scrutinising an object in order to check it for any damage, I make use of highlights reflected from its surface and move my head from side-to-side to improve stereo vision. By the use of parallax I can check if objects are touching or not, but when I look away the image is *virtual* and consigned to memory and so I *cannot know its real state* until I look again.

In times of stress I often feel as if there is a direct physical link with things I look at, even to the point of feeling *strings* joining me to them from my eyes, as I have mentioned. So, if I move away from an object being checked, the string will feel like it is stretching like a rubber-band to then pull the object from its exact position I demand it remains in. Moving my head or eyes from side-to-side puts tension on the string that is only reduced and slackened when I return my head or eyes back to directly facing the object. With all this going on I have great difficulty moving away from an object I am checking. The greater I am stressed the harder it becomes and I often stay statuesque until my legs ache and become numb before my mind wanders or I start to fall asleep. At moments when I am unaware and not preoccupied with the eye-string, I can quickly move my head or body away before the string reforms and ties me again to the object.

Eye-strings are very difficult to control - and explain!. Strings feel attached from the object to each eye and my previous problem with them was a balancing act to try to keep them there, facing forwards without them slurring off to one side, rather in the manner of trying to balance a light switch at the half-way point. If a slur to one side occurred, then I would cancel it out by producing an imaginary slur to the opposite side in sets of four. At the point of balance and when my mind was clear without a bad thought, I tried to look away accompanied by a slow blink. This was the exact moment when a thought, a word or image would flash through my mind and I would have to start the compulsion all over again.

My enduring eye-string problem is examined elsewhere in this book and is different to the past balance problem just described.

OTHER OCD STUFF

I have never been comfortable wearing clothes, always being aware of some tightness or itching. Not wearing pyjamas in bed is the only relief I can achieve, although the bed-covers are a problem to get just right.

Defaecation seems to have always been a problem procedure which still affects me to this day. As previously described in detail, I have to be meticulously clean and ritually check the seat, rim, bowl, water and the floor exhaustively, just in case I have left any faecal marks. I never have done, but this fact can never convince me - I always have to check *just one more time* - and another, and another, until I don't know *what* I'm looking at. Because I am looking for a particular imagined mark or smear, this image is present in my mind's eye, and being weary with the endless repetition I begin to see my mind's eye image. An imagined mark becomes indistinguishable from a real mark as my mind becomes ever more befuddled with aching repeating doubt.

Throwing an object into a bin involves many repeated attempts to arrange for the item to lay just in the *right position* with regard to the other objects already there; rarely do I get it right first time. There *feels something sinister* about it not lying at the correct position or angle I want it at – even if it is out by just a few degrees of tilt or rotation. I need the discarded object with length to be at the angle corresponding to the hour hand on an analogue clock being at about eleven o'clock with respect to the bin looking straight on. Also, the top end of the item - the end furthest from me - needs to be slightly tipped up if it is longer than it is wide. These positions are for no particular reason whatsoever – they have just evolved along with the wrong thinking.

This is particularly true of discarded cardboard toilet roll tubes, which have to be creased longitudinally to reduce unwanted volume before being placed crease-upwards in the bin. A discarded cardboard kitchen roll tube has to be first torn in half and one half folded longitudinally to then be inserted neatly within the other half, because otherwise it is too long and would take up too much space in the bin and cause an obstruction, acting like an unwanted supporting beam.

Disposing of paper into a bin has its own problems for me. Kitchen roll paper towels or other pieces of paper are screwed up into a ball before they are tossed into the bin, and they almost always lie with the untidy hemisphere facing upwards. It is the rounded side I need to see upwards for it to *feel right*. The rounded side is heavier and inevitably turns downwards during its thrown transit by the force of gravity with the lighter bunched edges upwards, so I have to *place* a bunched-up tissue paper ball into the bin at a point on the surface of the rubbish that offers a small hollow to retain the bunched edges downwards. I think of it rather like a dead insect with its legs in the air; its *proper* attitude should be legs down! Tissue paper edges or insect legs are detailed and untidy compared to the rounded tissue ball side or the top of an insect's body – the carapace of a beetle is nice and neat, shiny, relatively featureless, round and not distracting.

Another thought I have is that the upturned, untidy edges up, balled-up paper tissue looks like a sinister cancer cell in the photomicrographs I produced at the cancer research laboratory where I worked in the late seventies. They look like an upturned crab (cancer, from the Greek word for crab - *karkinos*) with many 'legs' formed by the often ragged, tentacle-like surface of tumour cells as seen in cross-section under the transmission electron microscope. It is too disturbing for me to leave the tissue ball in this 'cancer-inviting' position.

I tear paper and cardboard boxes into small neat pieces which will lie flat in the bin and take up minimum space; this doesn't cause much subsequent re-arrangement, if any, and I find the tearing satisfying and almost pleasurable.

Rinsed plastic bottles are folded or rolled-up with as much air removed as possible before their lid is replaced to stop the air re-entering. I don't regard this behaviour as particularly OC, as it seems obviously the right way to pack rubbish as tightly as possible. However, I have not found anyone else who does this, and I wonder why – perhaps it is just too much trouble for normal people and thought of as an unnecessary waste of time. I guess they're right!

But I do believe that there is a right way of doing most things which I seem to be privy to. But, again, OC behaviour isn't the right way is it?

Other discarded objects have their own particular disposal positions, but none of these rearranging compulsions take up much time; the compulsion just appears odd to the casual observer. Because of this I tend to use the bin when no-one is about – I don't want to have to answer any awkward questions. However, I do usually plan an answer to any question that may arise due to my odd behaviour, hoping it will be taken lightly – almost as a joke if I get the words right.

If I should ever receive a comment as I repeatedly check my car is locked, for instance, I have planned to give a straight forward honest answer: that I am obsessive-compulsive, because I reckon there has been sufficient news coverage and TV programs in recent years for them to hopefully recognise the behaviour and therefore not to ridicule me.

Clothes are given the OC treatment: neatly folding them until they *look right* with no odd edges protruding or labels showing. Even the clothes put aside for washing are folded the same way, despite the fact that they *obviously* must be *un*folded and shaken open before going into the washing machine to allow the detergent water maximum access. Of course socks are turned inside-out before washing to allow the inevitable bits to escape. Does anyone else do this?

I am unable to chuck or roughly throw a towel onto the towel rail when it is finally finished with. Instead, it must be folded longways with the label end down and on the inside right so as not to be visible. With the label folded inside the towel, this concealed-label folded half is placed over the back of the rail with its open edges to the right, whilst the top folded half is folded forwards and over to the front. The front folded half must fully cover the back folded half with the back half arranged to hang shorter than the front half to preclude it showing at the bottom edge and the left of the short-axis near-middle fold edge must be exactly butted up to the left of the rail where it joins the holding support. Head and eye movements follow, parallaxing the folded towel's front edges to ensure they cover the back edges by a few millimetres at least, finally trying to look away with the *right* or *no* thought and trying to fool the dreaded eye-strings. That is my ridiculous, laughable towel compulsion.

I don't have towel rails now, 2014 onwards, but still arrange them precisely on the wall radiator!

BOTTLE TOPS AND CAR DOORS

Tightening screw threads seems an insurmountable problem for me because of friction-slip. As tightening the bottle top (or the nut on a bolt - Ha! Me!) encounters progressive increased frictional resistance, it will suddenly, catastrophically, slip to the next point of stability depending on the force used and the amount of friction encountered at the engaging thread interfaces. I will feel this sudden slip once – but I need to feel it *twice* (an even number) – no way will I get to four because I will have wrung the thread out of its intimate mesh and destroyed its intended function.

When I feel the second slip, I should be satisfied that the bottle top is secure and that the contents cannot spill if the bottle should topple over. However, just at the millisecond of a successful second slip, I inevitably have a bad thought or image pop into my mind as self-sabotage, and have to quickly release the top and try again. This is where I can employ my satisfying four times, as I try very hard in the extra time taken, to adjust my mind to be determined to accept that at the fourth attempt *double-slip* I will have no bad-thought generated compulsion to continue this pointless exercise of eventually destroying a perfectly good thread. This is all well and good, but if I have a treble friction slip during one my four tries, I have to start again – obviously!

The problem is this: I know I will panic as I tighten the top, generating a sudden spurt of adrenaline-induced anxiety which will ensure I totally lose concentration. So, it is only possible to succeed at this compulsive task if I happen to be in a relaxed, low-anxiety state of mind – which is rare, but feels so good! Knowing at which point to leave a water screw tap is a similar problem which is solved in my present bathroom by those wonderful lever taps with a definite off-bump feedback.

This OCD doubting way of sabotage-thinking is far worse with the awful, dreaded task of checking my car doors are locked. Not satisfied with the remote control locking with the indicators flashing in confirmation that the task was completed satisfactorily, I then have to pull the handles to ensure they *really are* locked, because the audible click and visual flashing lights only tell me the car doors are *virtually* locked.

Mercifully, in my anxious, reality-distorted mind, I have decided that I only need to check the driver's door and the adjacent rear passenger door to be certain enough that *all* the doors must therefore be locked. Enduring checking all five doors would be an exhausting, anxiety-ridden experience - too much to contemplate.

So, I only check two door handles that both pull to a stop without the door opening. I experience great anxiety at the thought that my actions are being watched from a nearby window and the ensuing imaginary conversation between the two imaginary observers going something like:

"There he is again. Quick, come and look!"

"What a nutter! Should all be shot!"

Instead of the preferred reply:

"Don't stare. It's an anxiety disorder I have heard quite a bit about lately."

I then initiate the compulsive car door handle check.

I use the word *initiate,* because I have to prepare for the intrusive thoughts. I know at this stage I should take a couple of slow, deep breaths and exhalations, but I forget, because my mind is only on getting this torment over and done with, looking forward to closing the house door to then try and relax and unwind.

The process starts with being able to confidently grasp the handle, just for the same reasons explained in trying to grasp the toilet flush handle: anticipation of touch, texture and temperature. After a few tentative attempts I know what to expect in that regard and then proceed to pull the handle quickly to feel the sudden stop. This I try to do in, you've guessed it, four goes, and it must go smoothly and perfectly as anticipated to be a valid completion. I will usually do this fine and then go to the adjacent rear passenger door to do exactly the same. Then it all goes wrong! I get a mind-flip of short-term memory loss impose itself: Did I really do that right, before I finalise the task with the next, last door?

Even though I completed the first door compulsion perfectly – and I know I did, I throw all that satisfaction and certainty to the wind and rush back to attempt it all over again – this time, doomed to failure. After deciding I have at last convinced myself that the driver's door is well and truly locked, with each of the four pull-releases of the handle having *felt right,* I then attempt checking the rear passenger door next to it. I anticipate this won't *feel right* and will be agonisingly compelled to start all over again at the first door. Overwhelmed and adrenalised with the belief that I am *really* being watched, I take out a tissue from my pocket to blow my nose. This gives me a little time to regroup my mind and to surreptitiously look around at a few house windows before my next attempt.

Checking the car windows are all up is a repeating head-bobbing process in sets of four to allow reflections at the top of each window to reveal there is no dark gap indicating it is slightly open. I do this even though I have not opened any windows.

Finally, after five or ten minutes, I give myself permission to walk away and into the house, feeling as if I am being dragged back to the car as I move away. If I am interrupted or feel that I'm not going to get this done this time, then I go inside the house knowing I will succeed sometime after midnight when I convince myself that I won't be watched because every neurotypical will be tucked-up in bed long ago! The relief is intense when I finally achieve the will of that pesky demon.

All these paragraphs to explain what virtually no-one else *ever* does. Most press the remote lock button on their key or fob with hardly a backwards glance as they are already walking away. Oh! How I envy them; but they *cannot be sure* their doors are truly locked!

THE PROBLEM WITH DRAWERS

Opening a drawer presents no problems, but closing it can be a frustrating battle of wills between my common sense and the power of obsessive-compulsive doubt. If a drawer contains clothes there is little problem, but if it contains gadgets and wires the line-of-sight eclipse problem becomes dominant. I imagine that the drawer's edge will act in the manner of a guillotine blade to cut into any protruding part of an object. The problem is to trust my judgement that the object is below the height that would allow this imagined shearing action. I establish a line-of-sight to the front edge of the object in the drawer and then move my head forwards so that I can no longer see it by virtue of the obscuring position of drawer's cabinet edge above the drawer. Then, with a slow eye-closing blink, I begin to close the drawer slightly, having previously placed my hands pushing at the best point of balance on the drawer front, because older drawers have the annoying habit of skewing to one side and jamming.

I must avoid any sudden movement to ensure that my carefully placed objects are not disturbed in any way. With a slow, smooth movement, the drawer moves in to further hide the object and upon opening my eyes I am able to blank my mind in that second to fully close the drawer. There may be many attempts at this, but when I am satisfied I can leave it safe in the knowledge that the objects have not been disturbed. I then gently but firmly push the left, and then the right sides of the closed drawer front to ensure that the drawer is fully closed.

The process of shutting a cupboard or room door when I am attached by an eye-line string to an object I fear damaging involves the feeling that the door will trap or cut the string and move the object on the other side. I have developed a split-second simultaneous eye-blink together with a quick mind-blanking to give me time to shut the door without dwelling on the string. Several attempts (four or eight) will leave me satisfied enough to leave it. Because this ritual is quite quick and not too mind-demanding, I am able to rationalise that it doesn't matter if something moved anyway. ***That's the feeling I want ALL the time!*** I so fear damaging or knocking certain objects that I am compelled to invent this system of checking, when in reality I am more likely to come into contact with it by overstaying my proximity to it. Again, common sense doesn't apply. My eyes, body and mind become very tired and confused after particularly prolonged sessions of this peculiar behaviour, which leaves me even more susceptible to the onset of another compulsion.

I regard my fearful need to repeat thoughts and actions until they *feel right* in the same way as others view the fear factor in superstition and religious belief, particularly scrupulosity. By *not* compulsively reacting to a thought or an image, I feel that something bad will happen, particularly that I will continue to have these problems for the rest of the day because I did not resolve the previous compulsion to ritualise, thus leaving it in a powerful position to reoccur two-fold. With a compulsion unresolved it is like wading through treacle to carry on with the next task and also makes the likelihood of another, different OC, inevitable.

My mind evaluates this need to clear the way before I can proceed as the path of least resistance. Usually, I have not the strength of will to confront the feeling and to ignore it, it is just too compelling.

At times when I feel really strong-willed and able to confront and even ignore these feelings, I am consumed with a feeling of well-being. If I am able to get past a compulsion and to not dwell upon it, I feel accomplished, producing enthusiasm that I can beat this OCD thing.

I may beat the next compulsion later on and feel twice as good, but this run of success doesn't last long because some thought or feeling will sabotage my continued well-being. Being able to receive a pat on the back with words of encouragement are very important to keep up this productive momentum, but I had nothing of the kind at home after my CBT stint, but I can imagine how good it would have felt to have had this support. At the hospital I have known this good feeling of occasional encouragement and the knowledge that I beat some compulsions, but I always crash and burn having to endure the devastation of failure on my own. My few months on and off at Maudsley-Bethlem Hospital in 2000 was a productive time for me. With the aid of speaking with the psychotherapist and determined willpower, I was able to transform myself from a bedridden failure to a hopeful person who was becoming adept at beating the OCD.

However, cognitive behavioural therapy is just a grand title for time set aside in a medical context with someone authoritative you can trust to encourage your confidence at achieving success using your own latent willpower. It is like you have permission to believe in yourself by talking about the problem, especially if the chat becomes light-hearted and humorous. By revealing your dark OCD secrets, so to speak, you have both part-opened the door to kicking the compulsions out! You must maintain low anxiety, vigilance and perseverance to achieve this. It is hard work holding that door open, but eventually the OC demon won't be shut in with you!

Previously, as my opening chapter describes, I had spent four years isolated and virtually forgotten in a darkened room wanting to die, and imagining myself as a sort of curled-up blackened embryo under the cotton-coffin covers. In only a few weeks at the hospital I was beating the obsessive thoughts and compulsions and later was asked to speak about my OCD and CBT experience at two OCD conferences at the hospital later that year. Nerve-wracking, but I did it!

During my hospital stay I became aware of colour again, which I had been deprived of in my darkened room for all those years - a vivid reminder of reality, especially in the summer gardens of the hospital grounds. However, had it been during a cold, grey winter, I'm sure it would have been more difficult! I felt as if a veil had been lifted from me, as if I was at last released to experience reality more as others do. As I have said, especially as a child, I imagined a bubble-membrane separated me from reality.

But I now know this is how people 'normally' feel with Asperger's and that it isn't separating me from reality so much as revealing a deep and detailed internally reflected reality, an introversion others don't experience, which, compared to the normal neurotypical (NT) reality view is over-complicated and disallows normal experience.

After leaving the hospital when my few months of treatment time was up, I was unable to have home support because of family rejection, but it was essential for me to maintain my new mood of achievement. Over the following year I slowly, fearfully, slipped back into anxiety-fuelled OCD. In retrospect, I am convinced my anxiety and OCD are a comorbid part of undiagnosed Asperger's Syndrome, that I believe is in my mother's family. It also explains my later social ineptness and interest in complex systems.

I applied to be officially diagnosed with Asperger's Syndrome in Cambridge some years ago, but was refused because I needed to have someone with me at the interview who had known me as a child. Then, in my early sixties, there was no-one alive to do this, and so, despite explaining this fact, I remain undiagnosed.

Being under scrutiny in a public place is very difficult for me to cope with. It is embarrassing for me to purposefully and meticulously scan a shop counter followed by the floor beneath my feet, moving my feet back a step for each foot to see, in case I have left my bank card or something behind on the counter top or dropped anything onto the floor – even though deep down I know I haven't mislaid anything; I suppose that I am driven to check *just in case.* I usually sweep my hand across the counter surface whilst concentrating to see if anything touches my hand or falls to the floor.

The act of putting away my cash or bank card in my wallet is a trial in itself; again it has to *feel right.* I am aware of the leading edge of the card passing the edge of the wallet pocket – a threshold problem again. I will have to repeat this act several times until I do not experience that dreadful feeling. Then, when the card is squarely in place and pushed in as far as it can go, I then concentrate on closing the wallet and trying to foil the eye-string to the card. The closing flap of the wallet has to eclipse the view of the contents without encountering the string. This demands me to employ my eye-blink and thought-blocking trick four or eight times until I'm satisfied. Before this I have to ensure nothing else has moved in the wallet which might fall out, even though I know from their positions and the friction involved in holding them in place that it would make it virtually impossible for this to happen.

All the time I am aware that someone may be watching me, because I desperately wish to avoid any embarrassment I would feel as an overwhelming emotion if I knew they had seen me. Recently this did happen in my local pharmacy, so I quickly reassured the pharmacist that it was OK because I suffered OCD and have to keep checking things! I was quite relieved this happened where I get my medication for OCD!

If I am taking too much time and feel others may be watching my peculiar wallet-centred behaviour, I ruthlessly, and with wild abandon, cram the wallet, card and sales ticket in my nearest coat pocket and leave the shop to attend to it outside or when I return to my car. I do this because the stress produced by an observer is greater than the stress of the wallet and contents not being checked to completion at that time. Oddly, I am not stressed during the time until I can recheck it in private until I'm satisfied and *clear* to carry on with the next thing. I may have to mentally resolve any doubts later, usually in bed, with an action replay of my *memory video* of the movements within the wallet.

I can be some time hovering outside a shop replaying whether I had said something wrong or inappropriate to the shop assistant, all the time fighting the urge to glance back through the shop window at the assistant to see if they have been affected by what I said or did. Usually I give in to this urge, hoping that the person doesn't notice me staring, although I try to get away with a furtive glance, but I need four or even eight glances. Inevitably, once isn't enough to satisfy me, so I have to weigh-up what is the best thing to do: whether to risk the person seeing me repeatedly staring at them (and then to *really* have something to worry about!) until I get a mental snapshot of them *not looking at me* retained in my mind, or to force myself away to dwell on it later – a dreaded number one in my back-log queue.

The totally illogical and ironic thing is that by looking to check so many times, what was originally all right turns into precisely something *not* all right and something that I would have to replay time and time again until I have lived through all the possible outcomes of this *wrong* action, trying to convince myself that the shop assistant thought no more of our encounter and that I would not have to avoid that shop in future. The worry can build up until I feel devastated.

Unresolved worries about what I did and said form a back-log queue in my mind and has to be dealt with when I can give it the full attention I demand. If I have just one unresolved event then the likelihood for another joining it is doubled, precisely because I am stressed at the thought that I already have one to deal with and I don't want another. The overall stress I feel goes exponential as more items join the queue.

If there are more than two unresolved events then I have to write a list of particular actions, phrases and key-words in each individual event in case I forget one and remember it after clearing what I thought was all of them. If this does happen I will have to go through the tedious process of reliving *all* of the events again with less chance of success. I often fall asleep whilst tying to contend with this task and wake up later with the dread feeling of having to return to it all again.

FANTASY DETAILING

I like to embark on fantasy mind-game excursions to try and marvel at the historical origins of objects - a sort of AS/OCD daydreaming I suppose. For instance, I may imagine where the tree grew which produced a piece of wood I am looking at – it could be a door-post, a table or a chess piece – anything wooden. I envision myself standing where this particular tree once stood at the time it existed prior to being felled. I look around 360° to see the other trees in the forest, perhaps with a backdrop of a lake, mountains and sky. I obviously choose the tree to have existed in an idyllic forest or woodland setting and not in some industrial landscape; after all daydreams should be pleasant experiences, especially since my night/sleep-time dreams are almost without exception, devastatingly grim, nightmarish places.

An anonymous grain of sand will have the same mind-created treatment. I imagine its exact location on the mountain sedimentary rock surface just before it is eroded away, finally released after many millions of years entrapment. I wonder what the landscape below was like from this lofty viewpoint before the grain descended in its watery containment to the rivulets, streams and rivers on its journey to a lake or the sea. It may have been blown aloft to settle elsewhere on the mountain before finally being arrested by gravity and water to start its recycling process as sediment on some sea-floor, perhaps hundreds of miles from its provenance on that rain-lashed windy mountain.

Perhaps millions of years pass as my little sand-grain descends in an environment of ever increasing overburden deep below the sea floor, perhaps with its surface in intimate contact with the surface of a fossilising creature, both destined to be bedfellows on their immense geological journey to becoming compressed, water-depleted and consolidated sedimentary rock. Tectonic movement at a rate of only centimetres a year, gradually, but inexorably, propel my tiny sand-grain along and up into a new orogenesis, to finally stand once again proudly surveying the surface of the land and sea far below its mountain, awaiting the inevitable wind-blown, rain-driven moment of release to be hurtled seaward in a geological blink of an eye, to again embark on that slow-motion journey over millennia back to the mountain tops. That is, unless its fate was decided by the wind to be turned to dust and atoms in a wind-blown desert far away, entombed over and over again in the dunes of time. The adjacent mineralised fossil could have been removed by a palaeontologist for their collection, dislodging the little grain.

The human time-scale is vanishingly short within the geological time-scale, but perhaps for non-time-dependant inanimate minerals it is almost of instant duration, because its 'time' is not measured by anything or anyone and time may not even have meaning outside of the human brain.

If *time is the measure of change*, that doesn't say the *nature of change* or on *what scale*. Galaxy rotation around its centre is an entirely different matter in terms of scale and distance to the millimetre movement of a sand-grain, but they share millions of years of evolution. And, if nothing changed, time would stand still.

My Toilet Roll Rules!

1 ***Toilet rolls must have the paper hanging outwards and not hanging against the wall.***

2 ***The next available sheet must be whole with no tears and the torn perforation perfectly neat.***

3 ***The length of hanging paper must not exceed one sheet.***

4 ***The roll must sit perfectly level and straight in the middle of the roll-holding rod.***

5 ***Failure to comply with rules 1 – 4 result in anxiety.***

Update: My 2014 bungalow bathroom doesn't have a toilet roll holder or towel rails – problem solved, wonderful!

CHAPTER TWELVE

STREET CONTAMINANTS AND WRITING THIS OCD BOOK WITH OCD!

Street walking is not easy because I have a terrifying fear of dog faeces and unknown liquids on the pavement, especially vomit and sputum. I constantly scan the pavement ahead of me as well as trying to concentrate on where I'm going and plan to go. Someone may think my gait peculiar and prejudge me without knowing what I go through just to do what most take for granted. I will have an instant impulsive reaction to seeing something suspicious on the pavement and will have to decide in a split second where to step next, even though I may be several steps away from the object of my distress. I cannot jump in the path of someone walking next to me, so I take the risky route without care for myself by jumping into the road. If I am with someone at the time, even though they know of my odd behaviour, they always react with surprise! I regard the fear of dog faeces and such like on the pavement or grass as a phobia rather than a characteristic of OCD because phobics do not necessarily have OCD. We may know the object cannot or will not hurt us but there is no time to think, *the surge of adrenalised fear overwhelms*.

Long ago, before we had a car, we would walk with the children to get about and I would ask them to tell me if there was any dog mess ahead - to be forewarned. Luckily none of them developed a faecal fixation or phobia because of my thoughtless request. Inevitably, when a child trod in the dreadful mess and my wife was not with us, I had the unenviable task of trying to remain calm whilst removing the soiled shoe and containing it in something – usually a hurriedly emptied carrier bag. Trying all the time not to freak out my child, the uttermost thought in my mind would be where the nearest soap and water was. My greatest fear is of nasty, smelly messes getting into the house or the car. *That is understandable.*

Whenever we returned home or before we got into the car, I would subject everyone to a shoe-check that I would meticulously oversee and ask for them to repeat, because I could not trust they were wiped and checked properly – if at all. I have to check my own shoes in a specially devised scanning procedure that involves standing on one leg in the doorway for support. The right shoe first has its toe and then the back of the heel scanned as if I was vacuuming it with my eyes, then the right and left edges. Next is the underside of the heel, then the bit between the heel and the sole where all sorts of dreaded deposits tend to avoid the self-cleaning contact afforded by the pavement and the doormat, and finally the sole. All repeated for the left shoe. The full sequence is usually repeated again four times.

Doubting and checking makes even the simplest of tasks exhausting. Writing a letter first involves a rough draft version, and then the copy I'm sending is read and re-read to ensure I haven't written anything wrong, rude, stupid or ambiguous - even the blank side of the sheets are scanned a few times. I pre-address the envelope so as not to press through with the pen onto the letter inside. Once inside, the letter will have to come out a few times (no counting to four here strangely) to re-check what I have written and that the address is correct on the envelope. Once the envelope is stuck down it may be necessary for peace of mind to carefully slit it open for another check. You can usually tell if an OCDer has written you a letter by the tell-tale neat strip of Sellotape along the top of a neatly opened envelope!

Posting a letter is difficult, especially if others are around. Anxiously approaching the post-box fearing hesitation, I reach to place the letter partially in the slot, always re-reading the address and checking the well-rubbed stamp is securely in place. It is the pushing and letting go that is the hard part because it is such a final act. The fear is that after it's posted I might need the letter back for correction or re-checking, or decide that I had rather not have sent it at all. After it is gone from sight I rub my hand from side-to-side in the slot to check it is empty of my previously 'lodged' letter. Then I scan the ground around the box. If others are around, all this is virtually impossible for me to cope with without adrenaline rushes and acute embarrassment. Many times when someone has appeared, especially to post *their* letter, I have pulled my letter out of its rest position in the slot with a hushed explanation pretending I have forgotten something in the letter or need to check the address. I finally resort to driving to a remote post-box to ensure less stressful success.

Newspapers and magazines are full of traps. When I see an unacceptable word, like murder, kill, war, death, dying, cancer etcetera, or a similar type of image, I have to blink as I look away to cancel its effect on me. Again, this will be in fours although I can usually finish on eight - odd numbers are sinister. Even numbers represent symmetry, a balance I need to put my mind back in to continue reading the article or page. Each time I see the same word or image reinforces the disturbing belief that things are *not right*. When I read text in a book or on the screen, I get stuck on some lines or words that may not even have a sinister connotation, and I have to blink and flick my head to continue reading. I am doing this now as I type and read these words.

Often associated with OCD is hoarding: the obsessive collecting of objects which it is believed may be useful at a future time. Electrical goods are my greatest problem as I update a TV or hi-fi, because I just cannot bring myself to throw away perfectly good equipment. However, I do try to find them good homes. For most of our married life we have had at least one room and the loft piled full of all sorts of hoarded items that are moved from house to house, much to the family's irritation. Most of these items are never looked at again, very often because they are too hard to get at in the piled-up room of boxes. I feared going into the hoarding rooms because I might accidentally damage or even knock the boxes and objects aligned exactly to my satisfaction, which had been so carefully arranged and in close proximity to one another. The irony is that it was usually so difficult and stressful to extract a needed item from a box under boxes and objects, that it was easier to just buy another; my hoarding compulsion didn't prove to be a good idea! I still have some of the same items dating back to the sixties.

WRITING THIS OCD BOOK WITH OCD!

Writing this book has been a mixture of enjoyment, bitter memories and almost *pleasurable* obsessions and compulsions.

Being AS/OCD I enjoy intense, complicated challenges such as writing, but along with it involves meticulous attention to detail, especially during the editing. I cannot tell you how many times I have trawled through this book's text looking for errors in the punctuation, grammar, syntax and continuity. However many times I check and recheck I still find more. I have come to the conclusion that every time I check through the book I will inevitably find more errors – or my perceived errors; perhaps things which no one else would consider an error!

However, this obsessive-compulsive need to check and recheck is a good thing; it is just what is needed before taking the plunge and sending it off to the printers. I sent my previous book – a novel – to the printers when I was convinced that if any errors remained that they would not be worth worrying about and that by the umpteenth check it was my OCD directing operations and that it was not necessary to check it yet again. What a shock when I received my real book back from the printers! After the initial excitement of thumbing through my new book, it soon dawned on me that I was so glad I had only paid for a few 'test' copies to be printed. For soon after starting to read through the story, I found my first mistake: I think it was an unnecessary semi-colon. I had an adrenaline flush and thoughts of why hadn't I checked it all one last time. Then, to my horror, the errors crawled out of the pages like bugs out to get me. What had I been thinking not to have noticed all these mistakes.

During the weeks of going through the text of the novel again and again in seemingly never-ending gruelling torment, I unearthed hundreds – yes, hundreds of errors and things I wanted to change! Not only punctuation and back-to-front sentences, but whole parts had to be rewritten and checked to resolve the ultimate horror of discontinuity.

I have flashing cursor counting problems which is a devil of a thing to happen, because during the editing at the end of a line in the text, I am never sure that there isn't an extra space lurking in the jump to the beginning of the next line down. Back and forth I go with the arrow keys to convince myself that there is actually only the one required space whilst at the same time counting the cursor flashes in fours.

The trouble is, if I'm not ready for my terminal fourth flash, the damn thing won't wait, and off we go into another set of four with me trying to prepare my mind that it will *feel right* this time around. At the flash of four at the end of the line, I tap the forward arrow key to see the cursor then flash satisfyingly at the beginning of the text on the next line down. But wait! Was that right or was I remembering a previous cursor-flash check a minute ago? So I go back again with the maniacal clacking of arrow keys until it *feels right*, hoping all the time that all the other dozens of times I have done this at other lines were all right too. I mustn't go back or I will never get it finished and may descend into temporary madness!

I call this pleasurable OCD, because I know/hope that in the process of all this checking and rechecking I am gradually becoming closer and closer to . . . dare I say it? Perfection! I think of all the times I ritually check things that don't matter, and now, because it *does* matter, am I ever going to bring myself to the conclusion that it's done and that now it really can go off to the printers?

At the moment I am not only still rechecking that first novel but also this book! Pleasurable OCD? Perhaps I'm not too sure about that one after all!

I apologise in advance for any remaining errors; in that way I have cancelled out my obsession to worry about it! Or have I? No.

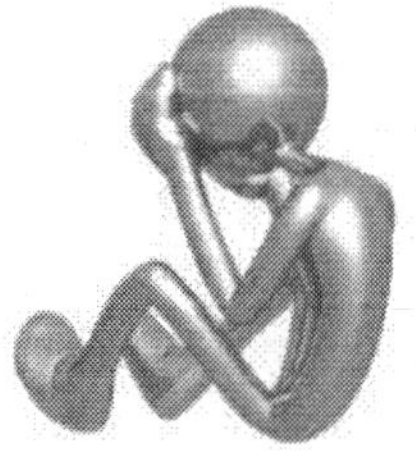

CHAPTER THIRTEEN

ON REALITY

MY LIFE and REALITY VIEW

My life has never seemed real to me. It is like I am an observer from the uncertain viewpoint of someone who has died or not alive, possibly how one may think of a ghost. Since my condition seems strange to say the least, my descriptive self-analysis can only seem equally strange to those of a normal ilk. I have spent around half my life in bed, probably more, mostly asleep, finding it difficult if not impossible to cope with the demands of *reality*. Reality, that is, as the consensus of opinion for the majority of people who all sense and interpret reality slightly differently, the differences being so slight as to be imperceptible.

As an extreme example, those who are deaf, blind or both from birth have one or two of the basic senses missing. The tactile sense takes on more of the interpretation of the reality around them and their sense of smell is heightened. *Hence, their interpretation of reality is vastly different to those fortunate enough to have their full complement of senses.*

I am certain I experience the condition of Asperger's Syndrome that has the OC perfection-seeking component, and my reality view is *very* different, or altered, to that of the average, *normal* person. It is as if the continual obsessive-compulsive rituals of checking everything is done to my impossibly high standards is my attempt to enter the *real* world. As I have said, all my life since a small child I have felt as if I am enclosed by a very thin-membraned bubble or envelope, unable to break through into the real world from my isolated state. Am I experiencing the memory of when I was in the womb and didn't want to come out? I experienced a very lonely existence as a young child and spent much of my out-of-school time wandering the nearby Grantchester Meadows between Newnham and Grantchester by the river Cam in Cambridge during the early 1950s.

At that particular time, I did have the sense of being at one with nature, but not with people. Misanthropy.

We do not all exist in *one reality*. We each construct our *own individual unique reality* by the information we receive by means of our five (plus?) senses. This electron flow of information is then interpreted by our brain into some semblance of order by which we can navigate our individual way through *our* reality. The images and thoughts committed to memory are our remembered reality. Further, our realities of the same event are *all different* and interpreted by our *individual* brainpower ability, hence, how one individual sees reality is always unique to them. However, enough of its interpretation is the same for most of us to interact with each other and the environment; we share *almost* common life experiences. There exists a seamless overlap in our individual experiences, enough to convince us that we are all experiencing life in o*ne unified reality.* The past does not exist *per se*, just each of our memories of experiences of it. History books record the *collective* experiences. The *present* is a series of *nows* - just moments strung together giving the illusion of time flowing - and the future is non-existent.

Each of our reality moments is hovering between our future and our past with each of our 'now' moments checked through from our unknown future to be confined to our past.

Exactly because our individual realities of the same event are unique to each of us and we all share an approximation of the same experience, we interpret this as a *collective experienced reality.* However, this is by no means the common rule which guides us all through life. *Some of us see reality in more detail* and have a far more complex memory system in which to store more facts - useful or not. Some of us over-evaluate our experiences, ponder them, dissect, analyse and question them. Those of us with OCD commit the experiences of our detailed reality view to memory, whether or not they are relevant - with *no filtering system* - even if they prove detrimental to our lives by popping-up as unwanted thoughts and images.

Great thinkers: scientists and philosophers, are mainly troubled people because the brain-work involved in keeping up their detailed reality view is so demanding and stressful that it is detrimental to coping with mundane everyday tasks. The *absent-minded professor* and the *mad scientist* are two expressions reinforcing this view. History is replete with gifted, oddball people who by modern evaluation had the condition we now refer to as Asperger's Syndrome. It is not something that is necessarily *suffered,* it is just a heightened sense of a very complex detailed reality, often producing satisfying and fulfilling insights, discoveries and inventions. It could be described by the well-known phrase: *'seeing what others see, but thinking what others don't!'* It is the extra thinking bit which can make it seem that it is suffered and makes ordinary everyday life a struggle with its perfectionist obsessive-compulsive comorbidity – it is a trade-off: mundane ordinariness for exhilarating extraordinariness.

To reiterate: *reality is created by the individual's interpretation and reasoning of what exists in the the world around them by their available senses and brain capacity.* Some see and interact with a very different world indeed; so much so that their response to it is entirely alien to others around them. I believe those of us with the label *obsessive-compulsive* are part of this group and most significantly those with *Asperger's Syndrome.*

I cannot help but interpret the world around me in what might be regarded as excessive detail; but is this an advantage conferring benefit or an affliction with negative outcome? It is an inconvenient state of mind to be in, because it is not the normal state of affairs, not the average general condition of the population in which interaction and relationships are to be successfully conducted.

Obsessive-compulsive people, and in particular those with the AS/OC mix, operate on an entirely different level of reality to the normal neurotypical person. This does not necessarily make them superior to others around them, instead we are considered stupid and weak and incapable of normal function. Normal behaviour is indeed difficult for us, but, as we see our reality differently to others, then we have no choice but to interact with it as best we can – ***it is normal for us.*** It is the way of things that we are questioning, doubtful, melancholy, pessimistic and downright depressive people; it is the price we pay for being *more aware of the complexity of reality.* If we were seen to be clever at something – painting, music or quantum physics for example, then we would be accepted as different but tolerable eccentrics and even well liked individuals. But if our behaviour is different and baffling for others and to *no obvious benefit,* then it is not that they do not understand, but because they *cannot* understand!

REALITY VIEW

Observers of differing intelligence, whether people or animals, continually go through the process of *realisation* to form their own unique reality from what they sense exists around them. By observers I mean those able to form a sense or an image of their environment from the information gathered by their senses.

IO + E = R Intelligent Observer + Existence = Reality

Humans gather different information from what exists around them than lower animals - a different realisation to form their unique view of reality. The greater intelligence of humans allows reality to take on extra dimensions, those not available or able to be evaluated by less intelligent creatures. However, lower animals are often equipped with different and sometimes superior senses: for example, a heightened sense of smell, and sight at different frequencies invisible to us.

An individual of little intelligence accepts reality *per se,* and has no interest or ability to look for deeper meaning and life is uncomplicated. However, an individual of higher intelligence (or sensitivity by virtue of emotion) observes the reality of existence at a deeper level and can be overwhelmed by the detail they extract. An anxious obsessive-compulsive person or one who suffers phobia, interprets reality with a different perspective and fearful intensity and makes conclusions based on this reality that others do not.

For example:

toilet = germs = danger = death, therefore **toilet = death**

thunder = lightning = death, therefore **thunder = death**

The toilet bowl is the fear trigger and not the likelihood of death by pathogenic bacteria or viruses.

Thunder equates with lightning - lightning kills, therefore the logic goes that thunder kills. Thunder is the fear trigger and not the likelihood of death by electrocution.

Distorted detailed observation and interpretation of a state of existence creates a distorted reality, albeit one that is true and logical for that particular individual. Distorted reality can be destructive to well-being when no logical reasoning can be attributed to the detailed analysis - it is an obsession with no positive outcome.

Attention to detail is time and energy consuming and stressful, but this is fine if undertaken voluntarily, such as a pleasurable but complicated pastime or a complex discipline chosen to study for the satisfaction of achievement.

Compulsive rituals performed to counteract or cancel obsessional intrusive thoughts and images are similar to superstitious belief systems and religious scrupulosity in that they have to be undertaken to magically cancel or offset the fearful consequences of *not* performing them - bad thoughts equate to bad consequences. Superstition compels the believer to be convinced something awful will befall them, another individual or the community, if rituals are not performed.

During early mankind, gods were imagined and created to be assigned to personify volcanoes, earthquakes, the weather, the harvest, the sun and moon, together with anything and everything which could not be otherwise controlled, understood or accounted for. The conclusions arrived at were due to lack of discovery and information about natural processes, limited intelligence and compensatory over-imagination. This state of reasoning is a completely logical process during ancient development in order to try and understand the reality of the observations made at that time.

The fact that this belief system still continues in vast areas worldwide is evidenced by the large demographic statistical overlap of poorly educated populations and of the superstitious religious believers with their false, misinformed concept of reality despite common sense.

This fallacy, this erroneous belief that mind can magically control matter and outcome by appeasing imaginary forces equates with OC symptoms.

The compulsion to touch an object so many times to enable one's mind to *feel right* allow the sufferer to continue the day's activities without the stress and uncertainty which would otherwise manifest itself.

Completing a task *with or without* certain thoughts or images would be the normal, sensible and logical route. Not believing one's eyes to be convinced that an action has been done correctly or not, such as locking a door or checking lights and gas taps are off, are symptoms of this aptly named *doubting disease.*

I think of it as if I compulsively sabotage my memory of what I have just done for reasons I don't understand and repetition of the actions only serves to diminish the quality of the memory.

Avoidance of these stressful compulsion-generating situations result in withdrawal from facing these tasks and reclusion inevitably sets in - and finally to bed. To counter this problem it is necessary to re-evaluate the reality perceived.

Exposing the OC person to a different reality from the one erroneously believed, a reality that is nearer the ideal to cope with and enjoy life, will offer the sufferer an alternative truth. As this exposure therapy continues, the successful person will eventually not believe they were ever dominated by their previous concept of reality.

CHAPTER FOURTEEN

DEFY THE DEMON

Many stumbling blocks throughout life are the inability to accept change and then to cope with it. When an individual is very young the process of change takes place quickly and sets a pattern or trend for the future which determines their ability to accept changes occurring in their life. The length of time necessary for transitions from one state to another are all important: the longer it takes, the harder it is to flow smoothly through life without stressful wrenching jolts.

When stress occurs for any reason and cannot be dealt with quickly, the build-up of stress-related symptoms become a detrimental template for future well-being - a negative foundation. Episodes of stress and their related symptoms and resolutions are a regular occurrence and a normal process to be dealt with throughout life. It is how adept we are at overcoming set-backs to the ideal flow of events during life that determines whether we are becoming a laid-back type of person or an habitual worrier. A person must not be too easy-going nor a long-term worrier and a balance must be achieved that can be a constant battle through life to keep within the bounds of reason; some find this easier to do than others.

Obsessive-Compulsive Disorder is characterised by an imbalance tending towards a negative outlook worrier, where a state of mental turmoil develops which disables the individual's ability to manage dealing with problem-solving quickly, if at all. A strength must be drawn upon to re-instate the mind to that of acceptable equilibrium - a coping strategy. But with increased accumulated stress this becomes harder and harder to do, and eventually impossible for the person to achieve on their own as intrusive thoughts and unreasonable compulsive rituals develop as a response to the mind trying to resolve this stress, exponentially worsening the condition until the brain can no longer function in a logical manner.

With a strong will and determination the person can *unlearn* ingrained negative thought processes and be able to reconstruct the brain's neural network in a positive way - a return to more lateral thinking. The development of OC *wrong thinking* takes a long time to learn, but fortunately it need only be a matter of months before the positive effects of exposure therapy are seen and maintained as I experienced at Maudsley-Bethlem hospital in the summer of 2000.

The momentum of positive change must be encouraged and reinforced by the means of repetition and vigilance of therapy. As this process of habituation continues by exposure to the causes and triggers of the stress - typically over-exposure - the person begins to realise that the time previously taken up by compulsive ritualising has now been replaced by exhilarating free time and an *increased ability for common-sense to prevail.*

I find the free time made available by overcoming compulsions becomes an addictive, pleasurable experience in itself - one to be repeated by eliminating another.

In the meantime, the person is encouraged to make use of this new found time to enjoy pleasurable pursuits, hence the vital part played by occupational therapy. Occupying the mind enables the person to live more in the here and now, tending to stop obsessive thoughts, compulsions and rumination becoming intrusive. *The more enthusiasm generated by this diversion of the mind, the less important the compulsive rituals then become.* As this feeling of freedom is discovered, or uncovered, by eliminating the time-consuming compulsive rituals and replacing them with positive enjoyable time-usage, the more the person likes this feeling and gradually the compulsive rituals are seen for what they are - unproductive and hideously boring! Soon the pleasurable pursuits become engaging and the quicker any remaining obsessive thoughts, fears and compulsive rituals become eliminated to make even more quality time available, thus making life worth living after all. *This has often been my experience, but it requires a constant daily battle of willpower with minimal anxiety to maintain.*

This dark enemy must be defeated by being ignored by strength of will to defy the 'demon' and then peace, calm and sense of worth emerge.

CHAPTER FIFTEEN

BELIEF SYSTEMS AND MAGICAL THINKING OF OBSESSIVE – COMPULSIVE BEHAVIOUR

In ancient days when scientific reasoning had not yet developed, strange behaviour was associated with demonic possession, it being the only reasonable explanation. The demon entered the person's body through their orifices and the resulting convulsions and fits were the evidence that the demon had taken up residence. OCD, Tourette's Syndrome, bipolar disorder, epilepsy and autistic spectrum disorders are familiar to us, but to people only a hundred years ago, and even today, this behaviour was so terrifying as to convince the observers that it could only be the result of the person's body being taken over by an evil spirit. Why this was the reasoning would easily be answered by remembering something the person had done, however innocent, which could be thought of as unusual, suspect, odd, unreasonable or considered evil because the demon possession of the body was entirely evident for all to see.

The fear of the unknown in these unenlightened times generated paranormal belief systems and superstitions as a means to control uncertainty and natural disasters by magical thinking.

Religious ritual compulsions are thoughts or actions which are seen to be doing *something* rather than *nothing* in response to obsessional fear. When the rituals, such as praying or sacrifice appear to work, it reinforces the belief that they were necessary and evidently beneficial. When they fail, it is because the ritual was not enacted with enough fervour, conviction or perfection, or that the sacrifice was *not good enough* to appease the relevant god and needed an animal to be replaced by a human - then a more precious human such as a virgin or a child if that didn't work. Of course, whilst these time-consuming sacrifices were going on, the causal reason for the praying and compulsive murderous cancelling rituals had resolved itself naturally and is erroneously seen to be conclusive and definite proof that they were entirely necessary: the ensuing rain had been granted by the sky god for the child sacrifice because the virgin wasn't good enough, or the bad spirit of disease had been removed by the appeased god of wellbeing, etcetera.

Along with descriptions and images of benevolent gods, malevolent devils and demons were invented, and *more importantly drawn,* as horrible nightmarish monsters to be the agency by which misfortune befell the individual who dared think it was all a contrived nonsense. These images are powerful control devices and easily remembered, to be conjured in the mind's eye as a warning. Artists had free reign to represent these fantasy creatures in as many twisted and terrifying guises as their imaginations allowed.

Before scientific enlightenment opened people's mind to the truth, this was believed to be the only reasonable explanation: upset the gods and they'll send their demons (into your mind) to prove they exist! Hence, the nightmares and persistent fear of not praying properly or gesticulating and posturing correctly, for it is a sure way to conjure up these delusions in the minds of those predisposed to it. Their anxiety, imagination and fear combine to convince them that these dreadful consequences will happen if they do not conform, and direct them to take the path of least resistance – to continue with their bizarre behaviour rather than dare to decide for themselves despite innate common sense – OCD.

It is unnecessary self-inflicted torture (scrupulosity) for religious believers to force themselves to compulsively ritualise, posture and pray without a blasphemous thought or vision and then have to repeat the ritual over and over again *without* this unwanted and unbidden interruption to get it perfect.

Trying desperately to cancel the bad obsessive thoughts and images with repeated physical actions or good thoughts results in mental disorder and illness. This driving OC fear is uncertainty.

Despite exhaustion, gross anxiety and fear of not *doing it right,* this religious compulsive ritual must be a *real* hell, with the increasing terrifying conviction that your god knows exactly what you have thought or visualised which cannot be undone, so you might be going to Hell anyway!

So, it is clear that delusional religious belief predisposes believers to obsessive-compulsive behaviour driven by fear and anxiety, and often destructive mass hysteria where extreme compulsions can be an evil illness – a psychopathy to persecute unbelievers and those of differing beliefs alike, without recourse to any semblance of common sense.

Enlightened by scientific endeavour as to how things *really* are in the *real* world today, we are still burdened by religious belief systems, resulting in stress, anxiety and inhuman ungodly acts of violence.

STRAIGHT LINES AND CACOPHONY

In this modern world we are exposed to the perfection of massed-produced products that appear perfect, identical, symmetrical and correct, in stark contrast to craftsmen produced objects with their own unique imperfections. Art Nouveau designs tend to blend 'imperfection' within their depictions of the natural world, whilst Art Deco returns to more rigid symmetry.

Increased stress has become more evident in the busy urban population exposed to straight lines, right-angles and cacophony. Stress induces anxiety, which in turn reduces the mind's ability to reason and to apply common sense. It is no wonder that city people retreat to the parks and green spaces at lunchtime, away from the right-angles of buildings and the noise of people and machines to seek reassurance of how the world should be and to recharge their minds ready to endure the afternoon's sensory onslaught.

Depressing grey replaced by invigorating green; disorientating urban cacophony by calm rural ambience.

Nature: trees and grass with twigs, leaves and soil underfoot – sound-absorbing, accommodating, welcoming and caring.

Urban: walls of buildings, concrete and tarmac underfoot – reverberating and echoic, harsh, unforgiving and uncaring.

Now imagine an urban landscape of arcs, circles, arches, domes and spheres with no straight lines or right-angles;

wouldn't this urban vista partly relax the mind as the rural landscape does so naturally well? Smooth sweeping curved architectural lines, roads and boundaries are easy on the eye and the mind, reflecting sound away. Without curves, stressful feelings of being trapped in squares and boxes of rigidity and permanence are evoked instead.

Obsessions and compulsions have almost certainly become more prevalent since mankind evolved a more complicated thinking brain with the development of imagination and magical thinking. The modern, noisy, structured, rigid environment has manifested itself in such a short period of time that there has been no time to evolve to cope with this massive change. Reaction to urban environments is utterly different to the rural experience. Straight lines and right-angles are incorporated into the structure of buildings with their regularly placed rectangular windows, doors, corridors and cuboid rooms with their eight corners of claustrophobic three converging right-angles, and street grid layouts of never-ending ninety degree experiences imposed upon us.

Dominant urban cubism and lineation are a troubling replacement for the gentle aesthetic shapes and contours of nature. What was easy on the eye and the mind became rigid, sinister and uncertain. The lazy, unhurried ambience of the rural idyll of birdsong, wind-rustled trees and trickling stream water replaced by the urban cacophony of machines and worker's urgent chatter. As the insidious, unrelenting, headlong decent into the urban environment and close-quarter living increased, especially during the Industrial Revolution, so did anxiety-inducing stress, feeding the fast becoming obsessional tendencies of the increasingly susceptible population, eager for escape into an alternative existence dominated by alcohol and drugs.

We have become artificially conditioned to believe that objects and things should be straight, symmetrical, level and central, because that is the reference standard provided by virtually everything we see and experience in the urban environment. If, in our personal, controllable environment, we see something which disobeys this perceived rule we feel the impulsive need to correct it – to adjust and straighten the object to regain equilibrium, order and control once again.

When we are in the countryside we never think *'that tree ought to be straight'* or that *'the branches are not symmetrical'*. We *prefer* the interesting, sinuous and irregular pathways through the woods to a boring dead-straight urban pathway designed to join places with the least distance. We *want* the clouds fluffy and asymmetrical. We do not stop to rearrange fallen twigs on the ground or those attached to the tree or hedge that *look wrong* or out of place - although I have had this problem with the hawthorn hedge at the bottom of my garden in the 1970s: I was unable to stop breaking off the thorns that I considered hazardous for the children and then replacing the disturbed leaves and twigs in a particular way.

I *do* pick up and adjust twigs that *look out of place* or at the *wrong angle* near my parked car, but I don't really *need* to. I suppose I do this because I *can*, and quickly without any anxiety, rather in the manner of flicking a piece of fluff from clothing as anyone would do without thinking. It's just odd that anyone would feel the need to rearrange or remove a few twigs! But for me, attention to extreme detail prompts this unnecessary impulsive action. I act on the intrusive thought rather than automatically ignore it like normal folk. ***My inefficient trivia filter doesn't respond to common sense.***

ASPERGER'S SYNDROME AS EVOLUTION?

Could it be that Asperger's Syndrome is an evolutionary response to this stressful environment forced upon us over the last one hundred years or so, by allowing us to shut out the noisy, invasive and demanding world to concentrate on technical detail in order to gain a survival advantage? OCD can be seen as the adverse negative response to anxiety-producing stress, but which is still evident as a comorbid component of Asperger's Syndrome. AS people immerse themselves in their own all-consuming world of passionate detail and can become remarkable experts in their subjects. Indeed genius has evolved to be manifest in some individuals for which society has benefited: Isaac Newton, Nikola Tesla, Albert Einstein, Leonardo da Vinci, Charles Darwin and Alan Turing, to name just a few.

I believe AS to be similar to autism with respect to its social limitations and tendency for isolation, but distinctly different by virtue of its propensity for heightened intelligence and genius - indeed a prerequisite.

So, it might be that OC behaviour is a *negative response* to anxiety and that AS is an attempt to resolve this with a *positive outcome,* although OC components remain. From my own experience it is evident that when I am deeply involved with my detailed interests, such as now, writing this book, the OC tendencies become almost dormant and the least troublesome than at any other time. (For instance, I am able to resolve the flashing cursor counting problem to the point where it can be quickly controlled and is demoted to just bloody irritating!)

I am grateful for my AS which has undoubtedly allowed my creative abilities - but I could well have done without its OC shadow.

If the AS type is an ongoing evolutionary work in progress to cope with the demands of the complex modern world, then perhaps the comorbid genetic OC component (synaptic serotonin depletion, if that is what it is) will eventually devolve itself to extinction or the gene be switched off because it is not beneficial - an unwanted side-effect of the obsession with detail.

The continued ingenuity of mankind can be improved by allowing the AS descendants to be free of its attendant OC limitation, hopefully with OC-only types becoming less frequent in the future.

APPENDIX

BENZODIAZEPINES

PSYCHOLOGICAL EFFECTS

Listed below are extracts taken from the Internet highlighting bizarre behavioural effects and the aggressive side-effects of the benzodiazepine group. I strongly believe I was similarly affected after being prescribed lorazepam (Ativan) to which I became addicted from 1981 – 2001. I gradually came off the lorazepam with the 'help' of diazepam (Valium) and these awful side-effects disappeared.

"Paradoxical aggressive outbursts are a recognised adverse effect of diazepam; they are probably caused by the suppression of mechanisms which normally inhibit aggressive outbursts." Professor Michael Rawlins, medical expert in court, 1980.

"A paradoxical increase in hostility and aggression may be reported by patients taking benzodiazepines. The effects range from talkativeness and excitement to aggressive and antisocial acts." British National Formulary, 2001.

"Benzodiazepines sometimes produce apparently paradoxical stimulant effects. Patients may commit uncharacteristic anti-social acts such as shoplifting or sexual offences, or become aggressive with outbursts of rage and violence. Some researchers have suggested that chronic use may contribute to 'baby-battering', 'wife-beating' or 'grandma-bashing'." Professor C Heather Ashton, DM, FRCP. Anything for a Quiet Life? New Scientist, May 6, 1989.

"More than a dozen papers in the literature speak of irritability, defiance, hostility, aggression, rage or a progressive development of hates and dislikes in certain patients treated with benzodiazepine tranquillisers; all those products which are widespread have been incriminated at one time or another.

"Unlike the experienced alcohol user, the trusting benzodiazepine user has little reason to anticipate losing control. Expecting to be helped, and not harmed, by the drug, the patient is less able to understand or manage potentially overwhelming feelings of anger or violence, or other untoward emotional responses.

"The benzodiazepines can produce a wide variety of abnormal mental responses and hazardous behavioural abnormalities, including rebound anxiety and insomnia, psychosis, paranoia, violence, antisocial acts, depression, and suicide." Peter R. Breggin, MD, Brain-Disabling Effects of Benzodiazepines.

"The implications of the combination of anti-anxiety agents and aggressiveness are astounding." D.G. Cunningham, D.G. Workman. Canadian Family Physician, Nov. 1975.

"Aggressive behaviour towards self and others may be precipitated." Berk Pharmaceuticals, ABPI Data sheet re: Diazepam, 1991.

Canada: In 1975, 81% of [prison] inmates involved in aggressive incidents had taken diazepam (Valium) and 3.6 times as many acts of aggression occurred in inmates while on these drugs.

This report adduces further testimony that severe withdrawal symptoms can occur with this class of tranquilliser and that lorazepam is, in this respect, like other benzodiazepine derivatives.

Any patient being treated with lorazepam should be re-evaluated continually for the development of psychological or physical dependence.

Minor tranquillisers, or anti-anxiety agents - the most widely used class of psychiatric drugs - also have been shown to create violence. Included in this category are Xanax, Halcion, **Valium**, **Ativan**, Restoril, Tranxene, Librium and Dalmane.

In 1970, a textbook on the side effects of psychiatric drugs already had pointed out their potential for violence. 'Indeed, even acts of violence such as murder and suicide have been attributed to the rage reactions induced by chlordiazepoxide and diazepam.'

On March 30, 1981, 11 years after this was published and six years after the Canadian study, John Hinckley, Jr., attempted to assassinate President Ronald Reagan in the midst of a Valium-induced rage.

According to a 1984 study: 'Extreme anger and hostile behaviour emerged from eight of the first 80 patients we treated with alprazolam (Xanax). The responses consisted of physical assaults by two patients, behaviour potentially dangerous to others by two more, and verbal outbursts by the remaining four. A woman who had no history of violence before taking Xanax erupted with screams on the fourth day of alprazolam treatment and held a steak knife to her mother's throat for a few minutes.'

Aggression and violent behaviour induced by prescribed benzodiazepine use is well documented and supported by strong anecdotal evidence.

As these and other psychoactive drugs are used increasingly in general medicine, there is a need for close attention to not only their clinical indications but also their possible side effects.

These drugs are also supposed to calm and quiet agitated and irritable individuals. Indeed, if you remember, when chlordiazepoxide was first introduced, it was publicised as being able to tame even the wildest and most ferocious of animals without reducing their ability to move about. The initial expectation, therefore, was that it would do the same in man.

However, even from the beginning of the use of the drug, it was noted that in some patients a state of increased anger, irritability and overt aggression was induced or unmasked. Because it was not expected, the phenomenon was labelled as 'paradoxical'.

When prescribing for patients with anxiety states the potential action of these drugs on hostility and aggression has to also be considered.

Anti-anxiety benzodiazepines have been reported to release bizarre uninhibited behaviour in some users with low levels of anxiety; hostility and rage may occur in others. Paranoia, depression, and suicidal ideation occasionally also accompany the use of these agents.

Among many symptoms that are common but less frequent, it lists depression and nightmares, as well as lethargy.

Clinical experience indicates that the combination of anxiety, insomnia, restlessness, agitation, irritability, nightmares and depression can produce a spectrum of behavioural abnormalities, including suicide and violence.

When depression occurs during the course of benzodiazepine treatment it is prudent to discontinue the benzodiazepine.

The phenomenon has been demonstrated in animal studies and it has even been proved possible to show in human volunteers that these drugs can release pent-up hostility, particularly in highly anxious or action-oriented individuals.

Whilst writing this book I found a reference to this marvellous work on the internet and ordered a printed copy.

Fred Penzel's book is compulsory reading in my view, a cross between an OCDer's bible and an encyclopaedia.

OBSESSIVE-COMPULSIVE DISORDERS: A COMPLETE GUIDE TO GETTING WELL AND STAYING WELL
By Fred Penzel, Ph.D.

Published by the Oxford University Press
ISBN 0-19-514092-3

DARK VERSES

The following verses are not a serious attempt at poetry.

In fact I don't really like poetry as so much of it is pretentious nonsense; so I will refer to the following as 'verses', which I only added to this book because I considered them relevant. Yes, they too are nonsense from a nonsensed mind.

The words presented here came into my head and were written whilst bedridden and ignored for four years, and during my attempt at recovery from a severe nervous breakdown, overwhelming anxiety and OCD torment, worsening heart disease, benzodiazepine tranquilliser addiction and deep suicidal depression.

Most verses are obviously pessimistic dark doom-fantasy and with similar themes and repetition. A few are optimistic, bright and cheerful, whilst others reflect my thoughts and emotions as allegory pertaining to the constant torment, anguish and hopelessness I felt at the time they were written.

THE IRON HEAD HAMMER

Steely glare on horizon fixed,
For truth to appear on golden wings.
Vast chasms of ignorance filled with knowledge,
We would all see these things.

Again the trumpet sounded from beyond,
Calling those from the wind of despair.
Ever deeper the cut of Death,
The Reaper takes their final breath.

Swirling dreams of spangled visions,
Fill the minds of those gone too far.
Dark obscures the grisly scene,
The desecration of Nature's Queen.

Tall trees of wisdom sway,
Warning those who won't obey.
Shimmering leaves on fieldly copse,
The Iron Head Hammer as it drops.

OCD: A Life in Torment

Trenches deep with sodden moss,
Silvered by the morning frost.
Slithering mud on greenless soils,
Mists of grey in endless coils.

Ragged lichen hang from trees,
As yet untouched by disease.
Dead branches hold these twin-lifed forms,
Against a backdrop of twilight dawns.

NORTHERN LIGHTS

On wings of the Northern wind the chariots sped,
Silver mountains, their cold to dread.
White to grey, and then to green,
Far beneath reflects the scene.
Mortals toiling in the field,
Cannot know what skies will yield.
Ancient lore predicts the day,
The Northern Lights will show the way.
For winged white horses to descend,
Life’s agonising gash to mend.
The mortals' tears, they fill the rivers,
Pegasus their dream delivers.

FAERY

In a brightly sunlit glade,
A magic spell a faery made.
The animals collected there,
To glimpse the faery's golden hair.

In the air she waved her wand,
And sprinkled sunbeams 'cross the pond.
To gentle breeze the grass would sway,
As little folk passed on their way.

Tiny insects seeking shelter,
Amidst the hurried helter-skelter.
As the moon began to rise,
She felt a longing deep inside.

She leapt across the golden pond,
And landed safely on a frond.
O'er yonder stood a silvered spire,
It was their object of desire.

There stood an elf with arms a'waving,
Jumping on the silv'ry paving.
A moonbeam filtered through the trees,
And brought the elven to his knees.
He prayed the night would treat him well,
And she not cast a wicked spell.

FOREST BLIND

Blinking, staring, branches flung,
I feel a song that should be sung.
The snaking creepers snag each step,
As if I have to repay debt.

This I owe and cannot sing,
Wishing I could take to wing.
To see right down among the trees,
And feel the breath of summer's breeze.

How can I feel myself empowered,
And not in darkness be devoured.
By the Lord of Evil strong,
To take me where I don't belong.

Sometimes a dappled light appears,
As if to quell my ingrained fears.
I see the light, but then it is gone,
If I could see I'd be so strong.

OCD: A Life in Torment

I'm startled by a noise above,
Perhaps it is a hidden love.
Come to me, Oh please today,
And then my debt I can repay.

I see ahead a verdant glade,
As if for me it's just been made.
What no-one before had seen,
May be clear within the green.

I hear a voice from the other side,
From the reality I'm denied.
It says that I deserve much more,
And not be on that forest floor.

I feel that if I walk on straight,
It just might not be too late.
The light comes blinding - the forest yields,
Before me lie the promised fields.

DARK MINED

I feel the air rush down the shaft,
It is one enormous draught.
I sit in darkness, cannot see,
When it's light perhaps I'll be.

It's cold down here and I will freeze,
Not for me the warmly trees.
A flash of light I thought I saw,
I don't hold breath, I just ignore.

I wait and wait, and wait again,
Hoping soon to end my pain.
Of noises here I am aware,
Is it help, and do I care?

Then all at once I know I'm dead,
Something that I thought I'd dread.
Never mind at least I know,
Nature's dice has had its throw.

THE DARK END OF THE STREET

I peer from the shadows into light,
I feel my life's forever night.
Up the street the children play,
But here in darkness I must stay.

Why is it like this for me?
I can't step forth for them to see.
Perhaps I'm not really there,
And that is why they do not stare.

I need someone to be my saviour,
To be free of stress behaviour.
The pureness of reality,
Maybe that which sets me free.

I'll do the things that I've not done,
And feel somehow that I have won.
To strive on forwards and in a glance,
Find that I have found my chance.

FADED GREY

Laughter now seems faded grey,
As for my sins I have to pay.
For what I've done I'll never know,
The pain I suffer seems to grow.

Dark and deep my rivers run,
Never can I glimpse the sun.
I grasp at flashes now and then,
It all leaps back to start again.

One by one the nights go by,
In every one I wish to die.
I thought my lady crystal good,
She did not treat me as she should.

Children grow and leave the nest,
I cannot seem to do my best.
Black ropes hang from darkened sky,
To tug my senses as I try.

I love my children, one and all,
Until the day I die and fall.
They and no-one grasp my plight,
I'm all but done - I've lost the fight.

BROKEN BRIDGES

Broken bridges, rivers dry,
The trees now dead and dark the sky.
Where mountains stood, now there's dust,
Nevermore to ever trust.

Landscapes suddenly descend,
Deserts start where deserts end.
Where life's magic once had stood,
All now bad where once was good.

Cackling hoards of demons roam,
Beneath the earth was once their home.
Rainbows again will never form,
Now is the everlasting storm.

Steaming vents of acrid fumes,
They punctuate the sky with plumes.
Sparks of iridescent fire,
Meets the darkness ever higher.

Where once was life has now been taken,
The hope of everlasting life mistaken.

BLACK DESPAIR

Bleak landscape crossed with much endeavour,
It seems like strides that last forever.
Trudge up a hill of hope, only to see another hill
On the horizon yet to climb.
Sit hands o'er face.
Black sun, grey twilight are all that lie ahead.
Loneliness.
In a capsule.
Can't break through.
Me inside, reality out there for my mind to traverse in a flip.
Oh, but only if it could be so.
Cosmos black, with specks of light inside my head,
No bright light for me instead.
Reclusive, bedridden, semi-comatose,
Sunlit mornings, curtains closed.
Speckled silhouette of leaves dance before my tired eyes.
In dreams I'm always lost, alone,
Filthy toilets at every turn.
Looking for her blonde hair* in the crowd.
Where did my world go?
It insidiously slipped from my grasp.

OCD: A Life in Torment

Drifting away from Starship Reality,
My tether broken - my only link.
Darkside luring me away,
From the light, bright sunny day.
Dwelling on thoughts obscure;
Looking for questions to find answers to,
Whilst I lie darkened in my cotton coffin.
No other way, only a coward's suicide.
Ritualistic obsessions rule every moment.
Dreamless sleep would be my death;
I'd be happy then, but not know it.
I know no happiness, contentment or relaxation;
That's what others wake up and look forward to.
Not I.
Switch me off.

* *Refers to my wife's hair*

BEHIND MY EYES

A demon waits behind my eyes,
Until it sees what I despise.
In a flash it leaps to action,
Giving me false satisfaction.

Why it's there I wish I knew,
From a childhood seed it grew.
It feeds and grows - thrives on stress,
The demon of chaos - his caress.

OCD: A Life in Torment

1964

When I was only seventeen,
No-one knew where I had been.
Three cold baths all through one night,
I couldn't make it feel all right.

Off to work in thirty minutes,
Now I know I'm pushing limits.
Sweating, pedalling - always late,
A telling-off is sure my fate.

I was deep in my possession,
Of this terrible obsession.
In my white coat, am I real?
Reality becomes surreal?

I disappear to wash again,
To face the Hell anew in vain.
On this issue - can't come to terms,
What to do 'bout all those germs.

THE MORNING'S LIGHT

How I fear the morning's light,
Another day to stand and fight.
This battle rages every day,
For something which I have to pay.

What it is I'll never know,
All it does is seem to grow.
A circuit in my brain has changed,
The state I'm in is now deranged.

One moment I'll be kind and good,
Then change to ogre, misunderstood.
I'll rant and rave without respite,
Unable to control my plight.

Adrenaline floods, I'm caught off guard,
To gain control is just too hard.
My mind it races on ahead,
I wish I could be calm instead.

OCD: A Life in Torment

At times I think I must be mad,
But on reflection rather sad.
Reason returns, my mind swings back,
Revealing the control I lack.

Drugs to calm OC I'm given,
But instead my mind is driven,
Not for better, but for worse,
The almighty benzo curse.

In retrospect I can't conceive,
How my mind it did deceive.
To make me worse by ten-fold strong,
Normality, I dearly long.

COVEN

Underneath the rocky crags,
Lived a coven of old hags.
Beware their evil magic spell,
It will send you straight to Hell.

Tongue of bat and foot of crow,
What they'll do is hard to know.
As the cauldron starts to boil,
Someone's life is set to spoil.

Lovers walk the crags above,
Sending out the power of love.
This the witches drain away,
For their spells the lovers pay.

At end of day the sunlight fades,
No longer falling on the glades.
Now is heard the dreadful drone,
Of each and every wretched crone.

This verse was used as inspiration for part of the story in my book The Halloween Chamber and appears on page 37.

WATERFALL

Raging waters swill and spill,
Over ragged cliff-side sill.
A rainbow forms as light is split,
Now the valley's beauty lit.

Veils of white and shining grey,
Reveal the mirrored water's way.
Channelled down from high mountains,
Now explodes in foaming fountains.

Turmoil, chaos at its base,
As far away the waters race.
Swirling eddies form with ease,
As if the anger to appease.

After tumultuous descent,
The water slows as it is meant.
The flow now smooth and peacefully,
The river finds its place - the sea.

DEW PATCH

From a patch of morning dew,
Came a promise that was true.
The dew transformed into delight,
The leaf stood firm and shone so bright.

As first of faeries, she had powers,
To tend small creatures and the flowers.
Cloned into a thousand-fold,
They more precious than even gold.

Spreading happiness into the light,
These small creatures took to flight.
Calming souls when in distress,
With a flick of golden tress.

Ethereal, but glimpsed by some,
As their work was gently done.
Pure beauty personified,
One for every tear we've cried.

FOREST DOOR

Just beneath the forest floor,
Lies a secret wooden door.
Dank stone steps lead down steep,
Underneath this forest deep.

Did no-one know that it existed?
Next to an oak, all gnarled and twisted.
One man knew that it was there,
But speak of it he did not dare.

In times of old there stood a dwelling,
Only known in folk-lore telling.
At the inn they'd often talk,
About a lonely forest walk.

Where it lead was speculation,
An evil place of desecration?
The man who dare not say a word,
Knew that it was not absurd.

OCD: A Life in Torment

He was descended from a crone,
To she and others this was home.
Witches, warlocks lived within,
To conjure up the Beast of Sin.

Like those before, a witch's curse,
Had sealed his lips, set into verse.
It spoke of tunnels to the past,
A time that was forever vast.

Long ago this place was fired,
But kept the secret so desired.
Blackened wood then fell to dust,
The doorway hidden - as it must.

GARGOYLES

Catch the eternal stone eye's glare,
Only do this if you dare.
The risk for you will surely grow,
As then its evil past you'll know.

Once a landscape bright and good,
In this place a long time stood.
The Evil Master's blackened hand,
Swept across and changed this land.

Devil dragon-dogs were made,
From the angels who had stayed.
Defiant were they in their stand,
Determined to protect the land.

These hideous forms then hid in rocks,
Later to be born as blocks.
Carved into the world once more,
Risen again to wage their war.

GOD'S SMILE

Satan lurks behind God's smile,
Waiting for things to defile.
Demons of doom are close at hand,
Then Hellish fire will sweep the land.

Satan sees all through God's eyes,
Views the scenes he does despise.
Images of light and dark,
The light now stands alone and stark.

Sickness spreads to those who sleep,
Love is shallow, never deep.
At the mushroom cloud they'll cower,
It is proof of Satan's power.

Atomised - atomic dust,
There to satisfy his lust.
People dying and in death,
Contribute to Satan's breath.

OCD: A Life in Torment

Forever blowin' 'cross the land,
Does the bidding of his hand.
Satan laughs as men lay dying,
As dreams of life dissolve to crying.

As the shadows move among them,
Men of blood he does condemn.
Things amiss are Satan's seed,
Gathered up to sate his greed.

Darkness once again defiles,
As the Prince of Darkness smiles.
Hope for Man has almost gone,
Impaled, they drip from Satan's horn.

This verse appears at the end of my book Cryptic Visions.

HELLIFE

Living a life is slowly dying a death,
It starts with every first drawn breath.
Creating reality by observing existence,
To slowly destroy it with our persistence.

Genetic freaks - the human race*,
A world we've thrust in Hell's embrace.
Hell is with us all our days,
But shows itself in different ways.

Each of us is sane in mind,
Until the day it's left behind.
Legions of good, we all unite,
One and all we stand to fight.

Determination, strength and power,
The enemy we will devour.
Never ask, I'm always here,
Never far but always near.
To make you strong, to feel your grief,
And to share our disbelief.

* *See Misanthropy in Dystopia (p.215)*

KRADLE

The parents stand and stare within,
The result of lusty sin.
The cradle holds abomination,
This evil they call miscreation.

Deep within's a darkened form,
Like the product of a storm.
An animated blackened vision,
The product of a lifetime's mission.

These parents are a special pair,
Lured on earth from festered lair.
Their reward? To be immortal;
Destiny? Time's elusive portal.

Now it's time to tend the Master,
Very soon to grow much faster.
The Evil Lord again is born,
Clutching from The Crown - a thorn.

Rosemary's Baby?

PERFECT VISION

The majesty of summer's fields,
All their beauty before us yields.
Clouds, they lazily drift by,
Cruising in the sky so high.

The smell of summer's grasses green,
The vision like a childhood dream.
Creatures' walkways through the hedges,
Into the mire among the sedges.

The insects, they move to-and-fro,
Along the little paths they know.
Village church bells start to chime,
For those who want to pray on time.

Children jump the babbling stream,
Running through their land so green.
High above the skylarks sing,
The memories of summer bring.

Tall trees gently sweep the sky,
The silver'd wings of dragonfly.
Rushing streams ride out cascades,
As the light now gently fades.

Insidiously the darkness falls,
Whilst birdsong still gently calls.
Shadows play among the trees,
As if guided by twilight breeze.

Childhood memories of Grantchester Meadows in the early 1950s

SEA OF BLACK

Deeper into the sea of black,
There seems no way of turning back.
Chaos from order, de-crystallising,
Within my mind that I'm despising.

I cry inside - I scream in silence,
Whilst all the world erupts in violence.
Where's the love? Where's the care?
I look to see, but it's not there.

The state I'm in, it seems more real,
Than the world I'm s'posed to feel.
Twin realities side by side,
Me trapped in the middle, deep down inside.

To bleeding shreds I bite my nails,
I'm sure you guess what that entails?
I need to break the lid that covers,
The golden path to friends and lovers.

UNREALITY

My reality - it's just not real,
Not the one that others feel.
I think I'm caught within a state,
That for return is now too late.

Everything around me's weird,
Just the place I'd always feared.
Can't make sense - can't take things in,
Life's a wedge that's getting thin.

I am writing lists of lists
'Til they fall from shaking fists.
Important things remain undone,
Where in my life hides all the fun.

VUDU

Ritualistic carvings hewn,
When cloudless skies and bright the moon.
Formed in moonlight, not the sun,
In rock and wood the work is done.

Lunar spirit locked within,
These artefacts can summon sin.
Carvers faced with confrontation,
Invoke the powers by incantation.

When the fire of Hell burns bright,
Their enemies no longer fight.
Instead, in yellow hues they flare,
In disbelief, their final stare.

This power of spirit electrifies,
Crackling bodies drown their cries.
So when walking ancient fields,
Beware of what the soil reveals.

WOODNIGHT

How d'ya feel in woods at night?
Nothing there to give you fright?
What's that rustle over there?
Can't bring yourself to stop and stare?

Keep a path that's straight and true,
Know just where you're going to.
If you stray along the way,
Perhaps this is your final day.

CROSSROADS

Crossroads here, no-one around,
Nothing to see and not a sound.
Who'll point the way for me to go?
All I feel is panic grow.

Hopelessness, loneliness - all pervade,
I'm looking for that verdant glade.
Something to give life direction,
But it still evades detection.

Landscapes of the mind persist,
Surreality in the mist.
I wish my focus would come clear,
To give me peace of mind - not fear.

How I got here, I don't know,
Did I follow dove or crow?
Left, right, or straight ahead?
Perhaps somewhere inside my head.

PAGES

I write verses when depressed,
To ease the pain when I am stressed.
Is it good? I don't know!
All I know's the pages grow.

Like a thirsty man keeps drinking,
With my mind I can't stop thinking.
Words flow out, like diarrhoea,
The final word looms ever nearer.

Words repeated far too much,
It becomes like double-dutch.
Still, I'm writing out my mind,
My eyes still see, but I am blind.

How the hell can I feel right,
When the future's not so bright.
Always bad dreams in the night,
Demons trying with all their might.

VERSES

I need to write this down you see,
It helps me with anxiety.
Words on paper, out of my head,
Are now here to read instead.

The sands of confidence I had found,
Slip through my fingers to the ground.
Every day is ever worse,
Back again has come the curse.

I really don't know what to do,
Confidence I thought I knew.
I'm very quickly slipping back,
Veering off that wondrous track.

I've had my help, but still I fail,
Now the hammer's missed the nail.
Gone's the feeling I was so fond,
Someone wave the magic wand.

DOWNSLIDE

In a terrible state,
Too much on my plate,
Things I cannot handle.
If I get through all of this,
Then perhaps there will be bliss,
A reason to light that candle.

Being depressed,
Makes me so stressed,
Can't work out in my mind where the path is.
My bed calls again,
To help ease the pain;
Am I strong enough to survive this?

When I'm losing the light,
These verses I write;
They help me to pour out my sorrow.
Confidence eroded,
My mind overloaded;
Will it still be the same tomorrow?
Each single letter,
It makes me feel better,
Although I'm so alone.

DREAMARE

Images of deep despair,
Seem to fill the bedroom air.
Repeated visions become so real,
They change the way my mind should feel.

Although asleep, I'm in a land,
Where negativity's swept its hand.
I long for sleep, but then I find,
Reality is left behind.

In this world inside my head,
Are places where I fear to tread.
Although the doors they open wide,
I dread to see just what's inside.

I lie and sweat in great distress,
Why can't I ever feel I'm blessed.
Allowing help from powers of hope,
To drag me up salvation's slope.

ONCE I'M FREE

Then I'll look back on my life,
And how I once had loved my wife.
Even though some times were bad,
There were the good days to be had.

Mountains will fill my window view,
And I hope have lots to do.
Walking when the weather's fine,
And writing in the winter time.

Embraced in nature's green and blue,
I want to find a life that's new.
Lazy walks by splashing streams,
Will be the answer to my dreams.

RIVENDELL HOUSE

The house we live in has this name,
From Tolkien's Lord Of The Rings it came.
A place of peace it means for elves,
Now we have it for ourselves.

A ruined church was up for sale,
We felt this chance we mustn't fail.
Derelict and overgrown,
We set a task for it to own.

Living in a caravan,
In the graveyard best we can.
Six of us, and four cats!
Whilst outside, a pair of bats.

Crow-laden tall trees brush the sky,
Underground the bodies lie.
Inside this small patch of ground,
Lie the dead who's peace they've found.

Once rebuilt and converted,
We moved inside, where once deserted.
A spooky place, the youngsters found,
With eighty bodies underground.

Of course, in ghosts I don't believe,
Events that happened could deceive.
Cars arriving which aren't there,
Tremendous bangs they shake the air.

Something lived here before we did,
In small crevices it slid.
It still remains, and that is fact,
Our resident is just a bat!

We're used to noises in the night,
They no longer give us fright.
Other things have happened too,*
Your imagination I'll leave that to!

** After moving in, my wife and I and one or two of our boys, witnessed three very bright lights in the night sky to the south-east of our church house. One moved almost instantly to be beside another and then shot off at tremendous speed towards Cambridge. By the time I readjusted my vision, the others had gone. It was the classic UFO lights description.*

THE CUPBOARD UNDER THE STAIRS

The house was old, so it was told,
Dampness hidden by black mould.
Ivy creeps through windows broken,
Wind the only language spoken.

Abandoned years - a score or more,
Initials carved upon the door.
Enigmatic tales are told,
Of this house that's always cold.

Children walked a different way,
Not to pass when night-time lay.
Through a window could be seen,
The stairway cupboard's flaking green.

You can look in, if you must,
Through this window caked with dust.
But what you must not ever do,
Is turn the cupboard's doorway screw.

This verse is directly based on the old derelict church we renovated in 1994.

PILL HILL

With aching heart I long to be,
Someone that should be me.
Instead, I have a madman's mind,
The real me I've left behind.

At times that person does appear,
But then he's gone amidst a tear.
How can I hold that magic state?
I just hope it's not too late.

As I reach each distant hill,
I have to take another pill,
To give me strength to stumble on,
Or else that next hill will be gone.

One day I'll climb right to the top,
Of a mountain - then I'll stop;
Breathe fresh air, admire the view,
And set my sights on life anew.

Alluding to my years of Lorazepam's mind-altering addiction.

LANDSCAPES OF THE MIND

Distorted reality, a twisted view of life.
Endless pitfalls, mountains, walls;
They're here one day and gone the next.
Heightened sensitivity to light and noise.
The dreaded night stretches dream-laden with disturbing images
Towards the dreaded morning and the existence of daytime reality.

No-one cares. Distaste. They do not want to know.
Struggling over an endless rugged landscape:
Over mounds, rivers, ditches;
Through holes to desert voids. Indecision.
Others are impossibly rude and uncaring.
Me? Impossibly sad and disoriented.

Trying to explain how I feel to others who don't give a damn.
Impossible.
It is like reaching out into a dark void
With little hope of catching anothers' light of reason,

Understanding or sympathy, but never empathy.
Empathy only exists with fellow sufferers.
It is the company of these I must seek:*
Those who can understand how I think and feel, or how I don't.

Caring for one another, holding each other tight and saying:

"I know. I know."

For someone to know how it is for me.

It is suffering a tragedy together - a sharing of our mutual turmoil.

Helping one another through life's cruel maze.

A sharing of a kind of grief for the missed normality of life

and the living of it.

** I later discovered this is not true for me. Fellow OCD sufferers are like the same poles of a magnet - repelling - and cannot co-exist for long because their obsessions and compulsions clash.*

UNDARK

Internally reflected light,
Denies all of outside sight.
But there I am caught within,
To all around a gem that's dim.

Do we live a life that's true?
One that's really me and you.
Or are we minds just left behind,
Ones that you and me designed?

Create a pathway in your mind,
One that only you've to find.
Far along its length move deep,
Then into fantasy you'll creep.

You will find that Death caresses,
Infinite and dark recesses.
The cosmos black and never ending,
Receives the thoughts that you are sending.

Unbending time of hours and years,
Takes no heed of mortals' tears.
You are here and then are gone,
As if for you there was no-one.

MR. HYDE

A private Hell, why should it be,
That others are so blind to see?
The desperate conflict in my head;
They don't know I'm halfway dead.

Sleepless torture in the night,
Images I cannot fight.
Cold and clammy sweating skin,
Those dreadful hours, they just begin.

Something takes a hold of me,
Captured, when I should be free.
Darkened thoughts prey on my mind,
Why can't the thoughts I have be kind?

Swirling torment drags me on,
To places I have often gone.
Repeating fears I have in life,
Slicing sanity - the evil knife.

OCD: A Life in Torment

Mr. Hyde, how do you do?
I know just what you're going through,
Each and every time I pass,
Right on through the looking-glass.

Reality, it fades to grey,
Beckoning for me to stay,
In this place where nothing's real,
Where wounds just bleed and never heal.

Tablets now control my mind,
Concoctions leaving me behind.
Perhaps one day I will be well,
Far away from this living Hell.

WHAT I COULD HAVE DONE

I seem to others fit and well,
But on my plight they do not dwell.
Inside my head they cannot see,
But if they could they would agree.

As each second passes by,
On the journey 'til I die,
I wonder what I could have done,
With this life devoid of fun.

My wife and children, they endure,
A person searching for a cure.
The pills I need to keep me sane,
Add to my life of mental pain.

In blister packs the tablets wait,
To push me further t'ward Hell's gate.
It is benzodiazapines,
That control what my life means.

Great ideas and projects flood,
Into my mind - my very blood.
I write them down, each careful word,
And there they stay, as if absurd.

One day my plans I will unfold,
But alas, I'll feel too old.
My body's tired, but mind alert,
My plans they crumble into dirt.

Now, nearly 20 years on, I have written three books!

THE MESSAGE

The awful truth I fear is spread,
Out before me to be read.
The words I glimpse - avert my eyes,
I must not read what I despise.

Read or not, the words still stand,
A mighty dark and evil hand,
Waits to slay all those who see,
Who nowhere else have then to flee.

Black ropes still hang from darkened sky,
The demon puppeteer on high.
Some thrash and whip, whilst others tangle,
Your life to grasp and grimly strangle.

Again the message is set before me,
That tantalising final journey.
Straight to Hell go those who read,
Best stay on Earth and gently bleed.

SOMEDAY

I want to live beside the sea,
That is where I'd like to be.
Reaching deep inside my mind,
Tranquillity I hope to find.

A little cottage, garden too,
Just enough for me to do.
I'll take long walks and breathe fresh air,
And be at last without a care.

Then some day a friend I'll find,
She, like me, will be so kind.
We'll hold hands on cliff-top walks,
And in the evening have great talks.

How long before my life's like this,
Hoping for some times of bliss?
And when there is a stormy night,
We'll have each other to hold tight.

SUPPRESSION

I'm not feelin' well today,
I still believe there's Hell to pay.
Have I been brainwashed to feel good,
Instead of Evil as I should?

The doubts they come, they're hard to fight,
I'm not feelin' as I might.
I have new friends* who'll speak at length,
The people who can give me strength.

Always outcast in my house,
Just like a hunted wee church mouse.
I'm hated for just being me,
All because of OCD.

I tell myself that I've been ill,
As I take another pill.
Suppressing thoughts that I am bad,
I must not feel this way - so sad.

* They were not my friends after all – just a group flung together getting along.

IN THE LIGHT OF EVENTS

If the universe contains,
Some other land made out of grains,
From the dust which was a star,
Can we assume one's not too far?

Fashioned from the quarks of matter,
Time speeds up to make you flatter.
Tachyons that you can't catch,
Only photons could you match.

If at light speed we could travel,
Some mysteries we might unravel.
Like: does the universe just end,
Or does it very gently bend?

Event horizons keep away!
We'll feed no black holes here today.
We'd be gone in seconds flat,
And that would be the end of that!

Time is zero at this speed,
We must slow down and then take heed.
If we go on like this you see,
We'd live our lives eternally.

DOWN THE SNAKE

In very nearly every way,
Things are different here today.
A day ago I thought I knew,
As my confidence just grew.

I was reaching for the sky,
I knew I didn't want to die.
Now all my efforts are put down,
By my wife with constant frown.

She hates me in the house so near,
All of this is made quite clear.
She wants me out through that door,
My confidence now on the floor.

What do I do, where do I go?
The answer is that I don't know.
How can I expect the healing,
When there is just no feeling.

OCD: A Life in Torment

My targets aimed at now collapse,
Into this state I must not lapse.
I have some friends*, but they're not here,
To understand and feel my fear.

I know they're suffering just as bad,
My head just drops, I know I'm sad.
Perhaps it all was just a dream,
The cat that never got the cream.

When I'm outside in the air,
I hope to find someone who'll care.
To start a friendship that's all new,
Paralleling points of view.

Help now seems in the past,
I'm worrying that I'm failing fast.
Can I sustain the will to live?
And not to demons my life to give.

** The 'friends' referred to were my fellow sufferers at the OCD hostel, but sadly none were real friends as no-one stayed in contact with me. We were friends of a sort only whilst thrust together for treatment in an unfamiliar environment.*

DARKLOUDS

The clouds are dark becoming still,
Waiting for that chance to spill
Their poisoned rain to form the gloom;
I imagine this my doom.

The thought I'm bad inside is real,
At black altar forced to kneel.
I was brainwashed to feel good,
Instead of how I really should.

Concerned that help was just a dream,
I wake up holding back a scream.
Was this the help of which they speak?*
Now I'm back to die a freak.

I hope I'm wrong - need affirmation,
I'll still try - determination.
Who or what is really me?
I'm still waiting to be free.

* *Disillusionment after realising CBT and Exposure Therapy are simply talk-therapies to try and encourage me to use my own willpower to overcome the obsessive-compulsive behaviour; but only with low anxiety.*

DEFEAT

What is there in this life to cherish?
Only problems - then to perish.
Death releases from this Hell,
To finally destroy the spell.

I don't see the hope at all,
Just to try, and then to fall.
OCD has ruined life,
To separate me from my wife.

I think I'm better - then I doubt,
Because at home my wife will shout,
About the suffering I've put her through,
And all the things I didn't do.

Bethlem was a special stay,
Now back home the price to pay.
It's difficult to feel much stronger,
I cannot stand this life much longer.

Perhaps there'll be a place for me,
As chemicals inside a tree.
A tree is peaceful, not like me,
But none will live eternally.

It is only death which provides eternal peace by virtue of non-existence, so living eternally is not an option I would ever want to take.

DESOLATION

An awesome, torturous screaming sound,
Tears the air and shifts the ground.
The noise continues unabated,
Into reason not translated.

The countryside, the fields, this place,
All once held a rustic grace.
Now each machine transformed to rust,
Reddening the pale grey dust.

Here the mighty structures stood,
Providing all the land with good.
Now twisted metal all around,
Half submerged into the ground.

Constructing this was mans' mistake,
And almost all their lives to take.
Power forever was the dream,
'What have we done!?' - the final scream.

Misanthropy in Dystopia

I can understand the concept of happiness and contentment but have never experienced it, only irritation and anger at being thrust into what I personally experience as a dystopic world without my permission. I cannot tolerate the human animal; it is a false evolution hell-bent on destruction of its environment and sanity. I much prefer the company of other animals, trees, streams, intellectual books and nice objects (albeit produced by mankind) to pass the time during this torment called life, which I stubbornly pursue to my severe detriment.

I experience a kaleidoscopic cacophony numbing my visual and auditory senses in shops, crowds and public places. To be in a town or city centre is unbearable to the point where I am existing in a sadistic surreal world until I can escape after I have done what I went there for. If there is a Hell, then this is surely one of its myriad manifestations on Earth I have to endure through stress and anxiety.

Being aware of vivid cascading detail has its benefits for understanding better the subjects which interest me, but not when I have to continually and unrelentingly trawl through the endless unimportant details of life which I am unable to filter out or ignore - my accompanying dark shadow, the flip side of the AS coin – OCD. I have a misanthropic world view together with self-hatred and annoyance at being a part of it; a life enduring unnecessary persistent trivia and anxiety, trusting no-one.

As an Asperger's/OCD person, I see the details of the reality of existence but cannot differentiate or filter out the unimportant from the important, the trivial from the necessary. As analogy, I only see the waves, eddies and turbulence at sea level and not the smooth ocean surface others see from an elevated aspect, which enables them to skim over and through life's trials. I am the small wheel negotiating the ridges and furrows - the endless details of life, rather than the large wheel of neurotypicals who are able to hardly notice the road is rough.

The human race is an evolutionary dead-end, whereby increased intelligence and technical ability of this branch of the primates has exponentially eroded its erroneous existence. *(Unintentional alliteration!)* It seems that our constructive human intelligence inevitably has a destructive dark side accompanying it. Mankind should learn from Nature; no other species actively works on its own destruction.

Everything we have created that is now above the ground was once beneath it and safely distributed by natural processes. Sediments, metals, minerals and invented plastics from oil, created the buildings and the roads, the cars, aeroplanes, trains and needless junk objects which now persist to pollute the planet; collecting uranium together has led to horrendous radioactive pollution and annihilating bombs; burning fossil fuel has put the carbon dioxide back into the atmosphere from where it was once safely locked away. Discarded plastic products litter and pollute our land, rivers and oceans and have entered the food chain.

We are the authors of our own demise and perhaps for a good reason. Of course, the planet will survive post-humans, as it has overcome numerous catastrophic events before in its long and varied history over the billions of years: volcanic eruptions, asteroid impacts, ice ages and tectonic plate adjustment.

Our existence is just an unfortunate blip in nature's blind attempt to evolve successful living entities as we became too clever and stupid for our own good, with predictable results some might say.

Perhaps the evolution of the human brain is an attempt by the universe to model itself and become self-aware, but didn't like what it saw!

Evolutionary biology has endured for billions of years, but the modern human (Homo sapiens) has only been in existence for around two hundred thousand years as a trial and error process which has inevitably descended headlong into error. During only the last couple of hundred years we have quickly created a distorted, unnatural world awaiting nature's cleansing and removal from the planet. Within the vast expanse of geological time, it will be as though we never existed.

Richard E Harding, August 2016

Update August 2016:

Further deteriorating heart condition preventing me doing much physically, with the resultant anxiety and depression allowing the OC demon to take control once again, particularly the eye-strings.

EPITAPH

RICHARD EDWARD HARDING
Misanthropist and Writer

Lost in life never to find myself
Thrust into joyless existence
I persisted to endure it
Those memories now lost
Like tears in the rain
Peace at last
Stardust to Stardust

Other books by Richard E Harding

Available on Amazon

CRYPTIC VISIONS - The Summerhouse Project

A story of international Cold War treachery and murder, from Washington DC and New York to London and Moscow.
Acting on images collected from the mind of a comatose special agent, a young doctor and nurse team in the 1980s undertake the perilous task of trying to prevent the Cold War from turning into World War Three.
The supernatural ambience of a derelict Victorian summerhouse in an English garden holds the memories and secrets of illicit passionate love.

THE HALLOWEEN CHAMBER - Revenge of the Corvids

The abbot of a remote ancient abbey employs a professor of psychiatry to investigate the cause of a strange transformation taking place in some of his monks, who appear to have become possessed by demons.
He reveals a twisted, tangled underworld of satanic revenge from the distant past by three former monk brothers and their witch sister who escaped capture for their crimes centuries before by becoming immortal corvids - three ravens and a crow.
At noon each October 31st, deep beneath the abbey's mausoleum in the secret Halloween Chamber, they temporarily regain human form and summon the Demon of Revenge to evoke a miasma of insidious evil influence into the underground river tunnel that runs beneath the abbey grounds.
A bizarre discovery links the abbey with Nazi Germany.

Made in United States
Troutdale, OR
11/03/2026

56844657R00122